T0318232

A Primer of the Psychoanalytic Theory of Herbert Silberer

Herbert Silberer was an early member of Freud's Vienna Group whose work was unique and prodigious; yet, owing to his expulsion from the psychoanalytic community, his contributions have been dismissed for close to a century. Based on original documents and primary sources, *A Primer of the Psychoanalytic Theory of Herbert Silberer: What Silberer Said* recovers the psychoanalytic theory of Herbert Silberer, revealing its connections to philosophy, theology and transcendence, and examining how his writings were frequently compatible with the developing thought of C. G. Jung at the time.

The book begins with an overview of what is known of Silberer's life, before commencing with an exploration of his writings. Charles Corliss covers topics including Silberer's groundbreaking construct of the hypnagogic phenomena, the process and meaning of symbolism and symbol formation, alchemy and its connection to his major work *Problems of Mysticism and Its Symbolism*, the use of symbols in Freemasonry, and his influential understanding of dreams and their meaning. The book also explores Silberer's complex relationship with the field of psychoanalysis, including his opposition to many psychoanalytic assumptions.

Introducing and assessing the main contributions of Silberer's work, this book will be of interest to analytical psychologists and Jungian psychotherapists in practice and training, as well as to academics and students of Jungian studies and the history of psychoanalysis, psychoanalytic studies, theology, philosophy, and the history of psychology.

Charles Corliss, Ph.D., ABPP, is a Board Certified, NYS Licensed Clinical Psychologist who serves as Executive Director and Supervising Clinical Psychologist of Inwood Community Services, Inc. and Clinical Psychologist in private practice, New York, USA.

Routledge Focus on Analytical Psychology

The Routledge Focus on Analytical Psychology series features short books covering unique, distinctive and cutting-edge topics. For a full list of titles in this series, please visit: www.routledge.com/Routledge-Focus-on-Analytical-Psychology/book-series/FOAP

Titles in the series:

A Primer of the Psychoanalytic Theory of Herbert Silberer
What Silberer Said
by Charles Corliss

Jungian Theory for Storytelling
A Toolkit
by Helen Bassil-Morozow

A Primer of the Psychoanalytic Theory of Herbert Silberer

What Silberer Said

Charles Corliss

Routledge
Taylor & Francis Group

LONDON AND NEW YORK

First published 2018
by Routledge

2 Park Square, Milton Park, Abingdon, Oxfordshire OX14 4RN
52 Vanderbilt Avenue, New York, NY 10017

Routledge is an imprint of the Taylor & Francis Group, an informa business

First issued in paperback 2020

British Library Cataloguing in Publication Data
A catalogue record for this book is available from the British Library

Library of Congress Cataloging in Publication Data
A catalog record for this title has been requested

ISBN: 978-1-138-22519-0 (hbk)
ISBN: 978-0-367-60715-9 (pbk)

Typeset in Times New Roman
by Out of House Publishing

To Marie, Kimmy, and Nick,
My true and glorious 'altitude'

Contents

Introduction

Charles Corliss, Ph.D., ABPP

Herbert Silberer was in many ways ahead of his time. As an early member of Freud's Vienna Group, he was a self-taught, aspiring psychoanalyst whose formulations were novel and unique. Yet, unfortunately, they were frequently too unique for Freud's clearly delineated dogma. As a result, like Jung, Silberer was literally ostracized from this pioneering movement, and his writings were dismissed. However, unlike Jung (who eventually recovered, and actually shepherded a robust Jungian school of analysis), Silberer was emotionally destroyed, and hanged himself outside his bedroom window at the age of 40.

Silberer's theoretical contributions were extensive, optimistic, and some might say 'other worldly'. They were clearly grounded in his encyclopedic knowledge of philosophy, theology, alchemy, Masonic texts, and the nascent psychoanalytic thought of the time. Presciently, they reflect an aspect of modern psychology's efforts to wed the spiritual with the psychological. Even more impressively, his refreshingly flexible and expansive stance on how dreams could be interpreted, which honored the nature of symbols and even hinted at things more transcendent (i.e. the 'anagogic', which was lambasted by the Freudian world), is seen by many today in both the field of psychotherapy as well as popular psychology as much more accessible and reasonable than the 'disguise work'-focused, drive-derivative model.

Additionally, and quite fascinatingly, Silberer's work was surely influenced by experiences that literally transcended those of Freud and his psychoanalytic colleagues. Silberer was not only a psychoanalytic theorist; he was also an active sportsman, a sportswriter by profession, and an avid *balloonist*! In fact, his first book was not on the hypnagogic phenomena, nor on the anagogic interpretation of dreams (both of which he would discuss at length later), but on the personal glories of balloon flight – which he recounted in detail, including photographs, in his work entitled *Viertausend Kilometer im Ballon [Four Thousand Kilometers in a Balloon]* (1903).

One might say that Silberer's positive, elevated sense of the human spirit reflected his atypical foray into the heavens at a time in which Freudian theory was instinctually earth bound. For example, at the beginning of the Foreword of his book, he observes:

> ...modern means of transport, rapidly though they may be evolving, remain bound within the familiar old framework; they continue to *cling to the ground* [but the] airship, it lifts man out of this framework, it carries him upward, over everything that flatly stretches out below. Mountaineers describe a similar sensation. It is the sensation of what amounts to a *new dimension* to the average human being: *altitude*.
>
> (pp. i–ii, emphasis added)

As he concludes this Foreword, he optimistically notes: "...Perhaps the chronicles here and the pictures that accompany them turn out to be of general interest; I'd be happy if they say enough to the reader to inspire him to follow me into the *kingdom of the sky*" (p. iii, emphasis added).

In the current work, I hope that we can follow Silberer, not into the heavens, but on the theoretical trajectory he launched in the burgeoning days of psychoanalysis at the turn of the twentieth century in Vienna. My goal is modest: to give the reader an overview (as from the balloon), and hopefully a preliminary appreciation, of the depth and range of his work. By so doing, I will hopefully retrieve his writings from the psychoanalytic cutting-room floor, and give them an appropriate airing.

Our method will be simple and straightforward. I will select major themes upon which he focused, comment upon them, and in the process, *extract liberally* from them to give the reader first-hand exposure to Silberer's thinking. The reader should be forewarned that Silberer's writing style, especially that evinced in *Problems of Mysticism and Its Symbolism* (Silberer 2015), is at times obscure, discursive, and almost encyclopedic in his lengthy, extensive quotations of various sources. I have, in general, avoided such quotations, and instead summarized what appeared to be the key contributions of such authors, and noted how these related to Silberer's thoughts on the matter. Admittedly, and not unlike dissecting some of the writers of his time (e.g. C. G. Jung), reading Silberer can be like trying to trace a fine silk thread woven into a hodgepodge of different fabrics. Difficult, but worthwhile.

It should also be noted that Silberer did not set out to present a unified, theoretical model replete with logically supporting premises and corollaries. Rather, his theorizing is embedded in his exploration of topics of interest, and needs to be garnered from the sum of such works. As such, frequent overlap as well as refinements of key constructs are interwoven throughout his writings.

Additionally, and a possible *further liability* of Silberer's writings, is his clear respect for spiritual striving, and religious traditions in general. In fact, some of his writings occasionally morph into meditative, spiritual meanderings – which certainly incensed the early Freudian community of his day, and may be off-putting to the modern-day, empirically oriented psychologist. However, even such occasional zealousness does not excuse wholly dismissing his work.

Lastly, it should also be noted that the researching and preparation of this book was no easy task. In the process, it became very apparent that a comprehensive effort to locate, collate, and uniformly translate *all* of Silberer's writings into English would be very beneficial – since the 'complete' body of his work appears to be in flux, with elements unknown, and/or in various stages of translation, partial translation, or simply abstracted. Additionally, given the fact that so much of Silberer's personal life remains a mystery, an effort to uncloak the details of such a narrative might likewise contribute to a deeper appreciation of his writings.

That being said, the discussion will proceed as follows. Chapter 1 presents an outline of what little is known about the short life of Herbert Silberer. We will then commence with our exploration of his writings in Chapter 2, by looking at his groundbreaking construct of the *hypnagogic phenomena* replete with numerous examples – many in which he is the subject of his own scientific inquiry. Chapter 3 will shift to his very rich discussion of the process and meaning of symbolism and symbol formation. Relatedly, his fondness for alchemy and its connection to his major work, *Problems of Mysticism and Its Symbolism*, will then be explored in Chapter 4. Chapter 5 will present an overview of a special focus of such alchemists over the centuries, namely the creation of the homunculus. Chapter 6 will focus on an outgrowth of alchemy, and also a personal commitment of Silberer's: Freemasonry and its use of symbols – and will be drawn from a series of lectures he gave at the Grand Lodge in Vienna later in his career. Chapter 7 will survey what many believe to be one of Silberer's greatest contributions to the field of psychoanalysis, namely his understanding of dreams and their meaning. To do so, I will draw largely from the book he published on the topic (i.e. *Der Traum: Einfuhrung in die Traumpsychologie* [*The Dream: An*

Introduction to Dream Psychology], 1919) as well as the aforementioned *Problems of Mysticism and Its Symbolism* – the latter when exploring his controversial notion of the *anagogic* level of dreams. Chapter 8 will look more closely at the complex, entangled relationship Silberer had with psychoanalysis; and at writings that reflected both his efforts to comply, as well as his clear voice in opposition to certain psychoanalytic assumptions. Lastly, the book will conclude (i.e. Chapter 9) with an earnest appraisal of what Silberer contributed; why he should be legitimately reintroduced into the 'history of psychoanalysis' discussion; and what relevance he has to current developments in the field of psychology.

In a word, if this small book stimulates interest in the writings of this insightful man, it will be considered a success.

1 History and background

Unfortunately, biographical details of Silberer's life are few. De Mijolla (2005) states: "...Victor Silberer, his father, was a self-made man who ran a sports newspaper and a publishing house. A sportsman himself, Herbert was one of the pioneers of Austro-Hungarian aeronautics..." Silberer was apparently skilled in horseback riding, and other outdoor pursuits. Nitzschke (1997) adds that Silberer worked as sports writer for his father's publication but eventually joined a Masonic lodge and pursued interests that he found more meaningful, including mysticism and philosophy.

He was also drawn to the developing field of psychoanalysis at the turn of the twentieth century. In fact, on October 5, 1910, Silberer applied for admission to Freud's pioneering 'Vienna Psychoanalytic Society', which included Freud, Adler, Stekel, Rank, and other significant theorists. He was voted in unanimously with six other applicants on October 12, 1910, and attended his first meeting on October 19, 1910. Unfortunately, it appears that his enthusiasm was not very well received throughout his intermittent involvement with the group. Given the fact that nascent drive theory was the foundational metaphysic of the group's regular explorations (e.g. there were several meetings that focused exclusively on the meaning of masturbation), it is no surprise that Silberer's more expansive contributions were critiqued.

Impressively, there are actual Minutes, *Minutes of the Vienna Psychoanalytic Society* Vol. I–IV (Nunberg, H. & Federn, E. eds. 1962) for long stretches of the meetings between October 10, 1906 and March 31, 1915. Such Minutes highlight Freud's strong grip on the proceedings, and the persistent emphasis on drive theory. Possibly due to this, or for reasons yet uncovered, Silberer's attendance record was mediocre at best (i.e. he attended less than half of the meetings on record between October 19, 1910 and November 18, 1918). Additionally, as per the

recorded Minutes, his contributions during most meetings were inci-
dental, nonexistent, or not significant enough to be noted. Also, on at
least a few occasions, his opinions seemed to be indirectly or directly
rebuked by Freud or his supporters.

For example, at the April 26, 1911 meeting in which Stekel's book,
The Language of Dreams, was discussed, the Minutes reflect that "...
SILBERER stresses appreciatively that Stekel's book, despite the super-
ficiality of some passages, has served him well in the clinical interpretation of dreams..." and that he had only one minor reservation about
it (Vol. III, p. 235). However, Freud soon retorted harshly that Stekel
makes too much of symbolism (i.e. "...Stekel did not know how to keep
himself within limits. Not all dreams require the application of symbolism...") and condemned "...Stekel's overvaluation of the manifest
dream content..." (Vol. III, p. 236) – clearly deflating Silberer's attempt
at support. On the other hand, in the Minutes of January 31, 1912 (Vol.
IV, p. 32), Silberer (reflecting his early attempts to display Freudian
orthodoxy?) interestingly concurs with the presenter, Dr. Paul Federn,
that dreams about flying frequently have sexual implications, and shares
that he actually had a dream that fit this criterion the previous night.
Not surprisingly, "...PROF. FREUD is in considerable agreement
with many of the speaker's statements and cannot take issue with the
others..." (Vol. IV, p. 33).

However, at the February 14, 1912 meeting in which Dr. Karl
Schrotter presented on the "Experimental Dream", Silberer discusses
how in fact Schrotter's notion that "...man actually dreams continu-
ously..." can occur (Vol. IV, p. 48). However, the Minutes reflect that
Freud dismisses the notion immediately after Silberer's contribution: "...PROF. FREUD regards as unscientific the question of whether
there is continuous dreaming..." (Vol. IV, p. 48).

Yet, Silberer did have a few opportunities to present some elements of
his work to the group. How well this was received is not certain. Minutes
from the April 3, 1912 meeting, in which he presented "Spermatozoa
Dreams", and November 12, 1913, on which he presented on "The
Homunculus", are missing.

Minutes do exist from the January 18, 1911 meeting (Vol. III,
pp. 126–132) in which he presented on "Magic and Other Topics", but
unfortunately reflect an experience that did not go well for Silberer.
Although he received some nominal support for his theory of the
functional vs. material phenomena of consciousness, he was roundly
and harshly criticized throughout the meeting. In fact, Tausk sets the
tone with his initial comment: "...TAUSK would like merely to point
out that these interesting things can already be found in the material

that has been worked through psychoanalytically, above all in Freud's work ... Freud has already dealt with these problems..." (Vol. III, pp. 128–129).

The Minutes reflect that the criticism continued: "...FRANZ GRUNER remarks that the speaker was actually going in a direction opposite to that pursued by psychoanalysis..." (Vol. III, p. 129); "FURTMULLER reiterates ... that Staudenmaier (who Silberer references respectfully) must not be taken seriously..." (p. 130); "... ROSENSTEIN would like to raise the question of what the meaning is of these functional phenomena, since we are after all accustomed to assuming that the psyche reacts only to pleasure and unpleasure..." (Vol. III, p. 131), and "...DR. F. S. KRAUSS [states] Spiritualistic sessions (again spoken about sympathetically by Silberer) are nothing but humbug..." (Vol. III, p. 131). Interestingly and extremely rare, no comments are recorded by Freud throughout the meeting – perhaps reflecting his satisfaction that his faithful were ably taking the fight to Silberer. Although Silberer attempted in vain to diplomatically clarify his position on the material vs. functional phenomena at the very end of the meeting, it is apparent that he suffered so thorough a lambasting that it is remarkable he continued to attend future meetings.

What appears to also be clear is the fact that although the Minutes are not available, Silberer's final presentation (November 1, 1922) to the group was again so poorly received, and the criticism he encountered so severe, that Stekel maintained that this precipitated his suicide a few months later.

Thus, upon reflection, although he might have had a few promising moments, it appears that Silberer's overall engagement in Freud's Vienna Group was aversive, and ultimately destructive.

A richer, more extensive, and more positive illustration of Silberer's foray into the psychoanalytic world was evinced in the New York based journal *Psyche and Eros*, which he co-edited with his aforementioned colleague, Wilhelm Stekel, from July 1920 to February 1922. His extensive writings included a four-part study of the symbolism of Freemasonry; an analysis of the experiments of a Viennese biologist, Professor Steinach, from a mythological perspective; a discourse on the interplay between sociology, politics, and psychoanalysis; and even a bold assessment entitled "Beyond Psychoanalysis" in which he critiqued Freud's 1920 essay entitled "Jen-seits des Lustprinzips" [Beyond the Pleasure Principle]. Silberer also wrote numerous reviews of current articles, including: an essay on symbolism by Ernest Jones; a journal article by Freud on 'crowd psychology'; and various essays on subjects such as telepathy, clairvoyance, and mysticism. Two things are apparent when one reviews Silberer's *Psyche and Eros* portfolio. First, he had clearly developed a reasoned, articulate theoretical stance, and communicated it coherently and crisply – more so than his more obscure earlier writings. Second, he was continuing to stray from the Freudian fold into the world of apostacy – so much so that Stekel maintained that Silberer resigned as co-editor in 1922 in a failed attempt to maintain a favorable connection with Freud and his followers.

Foreshadowing his own fate, yet to his credit, Silberer remained true to Stekel even after Freud had expelled Stekel from the psychoanalytic fold. Reflecting on this in an obituary of Silberer, Stekel stated: "... When I separated from Freud, he was the only one of all the Freudians who remained true to me. (He was to pay dearly for this friendship)..." (Roazen 1984, p. 341).

Silberer's early (1909) psychological interests were in what was known as 'hypnagogic phenomema': the period between waking and sleep in which mild hallucinatory activity can occur. His opus magna was his *Problems of Mysticism and Its Symbolism*: an obscure, yet scholarly work covering a wide range of intersecting topics including psychoanalysis, theology, alchemy, and metaphysics. The depth of the work's scholarship was striking, as was his openness to complex, and at times, amorphous, metaphysical and spiritual constructs throughout.

According to Jacob Blauner (1955), Silberer also gave a lecture in Vienna in 1918 on dreams, and eventually published it under the title, as noted above, *The Dream: Introduction to the Psychology of Dreams*. In it, Silberer continued to bolster his position on multiple determinants of symbols, and the possibility of considering a deeper level when interpreting dreams – both clear irritants to Freud and the psychoanalytic movement. Perhaps such irritation was the reason why the book was only translated into English *37 years* after it was originally published, and even then, *not completely so*. In fact, it appears that most of Silberer's writings, if noticed at all by the psychoanalytic community, were abstracted, or summarized, or when finally translated, were *incompletely* translated at the translator's discretion.

In fact, although Freud reluctantly acknowledged the value of Silberer's writings on the hypnagogic, and advised Jung, the editor of the newly minted *Jahrbuch* journal at the time to publish it in 1909, Freud eventually communicated his unequivocal disapproval of Silberer's subsequent work. Freud appeared to have no tolerance for Silberer's notion of the *anagogic* level of dream symbols, nor the seeming metaphysical/theological musings in the above-noted *Problems of Mysticism and Its Symbolism*. Accordingly, Freud proceeded to let his followers know that Silberer's work should not be taken seriously. One of Freud's strongest supporters, Ernest Jones, soon echoed the sentiment, stating that Silberer seemed to have been "badly infected by the philosophic virus..." (de Mijolla 2005). Roazen (1984) even more explicitly details Freud's condemnation when he recounts: "...Silberer had been bitterly assailed at the presentation of a paper at the Vienna Psychoanalytic Society, and Freud was said to have explained the behavior of his followers on the grounds that *'the man is a Jesuit'..."* (p. 341).

Although there is some disagreement (see, for example, de Mijolla 2005) on this fact, Roazen (1984) maintains that the following brief note of Freud (April 17, 1922) was, in fact, written to *Herbert* Silberer (not his father, *Victor*), and accelerated his dramatic suicide (hanging with a flashlight wrapped around his neck) nine months later:

> Dear Sir,
>   I request that you do not make the intended visit with me. As the result of the observations and impression of recent years I no longer desire personal contact with you.
>
> Very truly yours,
> Freud
>
> (Roazen 1984, p. 339)

Thus, although significant details of his life remain largely a mystery, it is clear that Silberer's life was one that ended tragically, and that his many contributions were allowed to fade into oblivion. In an effort to recover his voice, we will first explore his earliest writings, beginning with his exploration of the hypnagogic.

2 Early writings

The hypnagogic phenomena

Silberer's thoughts on the *hypnagogic state* contained in his "Report on a Method of Eliciting and Observing Certain Symbolic Hallucination-Phenomena" (first published in *Jahrbuch* [1909]; then in David Rapaport, Editor and Translator, *Organization and Pathology of Thought* [1951], pp. 195–207) were groundbreaking. Like a true scientist of a bygone era, the genesis of his original inquiry was his own self-reflection. Specifically, as he was repeatedly attempting to grasp a complex Kantian philosophical concept that continued to elude him, he momentarily dozed off, and suddenly realized that this process was immediately represented *symbolically* as follows: "I am asking a morose secretary for some information; he is leaning over his desk and disregarding me entirely; he straightens up for a moment to give me an unfriendly and rejecting look..." (p. 196). Silberer labeled this automatic translation of thought into image as the "autosymbolic phenomenon".

He goes on to explain that his intuitive sense of the reason for this phenomenon proved true: i.e. the tension between drowsiness and an effort to think results in a spontaneous selection of a symbol that is adequate to represent the thought at issue. He also asserts: "I was impressed by the appropriateness of this unconsciously selected symbol" (p. 196).

Silberer delineates three types of such symbols:

* *Material (content) phenomena*: symbols arising in this hypnagogic state that are representative of ideas, concepts, definitions, judgments, etc. (i.e. items of cognition). Silberer's example is fascinating: "...In a state of drowsiness I contemplate an abstract topic such as the nature of transsubjectively (for all people) valid judgments ... The content of my thought presents itself to me immediately in the form of a perceptual (for an instant apparently real) picture: I see a big circle (or transparent sphere) in the air with people around it whose heads reach into the circle..." (p. 198).

- *Functional (effort) phenomena*: symbols that arise in the hypnagogic state that "...represent the condition of the subject experiencing them or the effectiveness of his consciousness. They ... have to do with the mode of functioning of consciousness (quick, slow, easy, difficult, relaxed...)" (p. 199). Silberer goes on to assert that: "...This second group of autosymbolic phenomena demonstrates that the symbolizing function of consciousness deals not only with the content of thought; often it is the mode of functioning of the thought-process that is symbolically represented..." (p. 199).

- *Somatic phenomena*: symbols arising in the hypnagogic state that seem to have arisen directly from a physiological condition and sensation. Silberer lists numerous possibilities including: "...temperature, external pain and position sensations, sensations of the joints and muscles, coenesthesias, acoustic, optic, chemical, and mechanical stimulations, and sensation complexes..." potentially caused by "...pressure of a blanket on the foot, itching of the nose, rheumatic pains in the joints, a breeze touching the cheek, palpitation, noise, the scent of flowers, anxiety, apnoea, and so forth..." (pp. 200–201).

Silberer notes, however, that the third category, the *somatic autosymbolic phenomena*, is qualitatively different from the first two in that: "...The 'effort to think' is irrelevant in the genesis of the phenomena of this group, and in the struggle against drowsiness the 'will' is replaced by sensations or feelings..." (p. 201).

Silberer then offers additional examples of such phenomena, including:

Material Phenomena:

"EXAMPLE 1. My thought is: I am to improve a halting passage in an essay. *Symbol*: I see myself planing a piece of wood."

"EXAMPLE 2. I think of human understanding probing into the foggy and difficult problem of the 'Mothers' (*Faust*, Part II). *Symbol*: I stand alone on a stone jetty extending out far into a dark sea. The waters of the ocean and the dark and the mysteriously heavy air unite at the horizon."

"EXAMPLE 4. I decide to dissuade someone from carrying out a dangerous resolution. I want to tell him: 'If you do that, grave misfortune will befall you'. *Symbol*: I see three gruesome-looking riders on black horses storming over a dusky field under leaden skies" (pp. 202–203).

Functional Phenomena:

"EXAMPLE 8. Before falling asleep I want to review an idea in order not to forget it. *Symbol*: Suddenly a lackey in livery stands before me as though waiting for my orders."

"EXAMPLE 9. I lose the thread of my thought. I make an effort to pick it up again, but must admit that I have lost the connecting link. *Symbol*: A piece of type-setting with the last few lines gone."

"EXAMPLE 10. I am thinking about something. Pursuing a subsidiary consideration, I depart from my original theme. When I attempt to return to it, an autosymbolic phenomenon occurs. *Symbol:* I am out mountain climbing. The mountains near me conceal the farther ones from which I came and to which I want to return" (p. 204).

Somatic Phenomena:

"EXAMPLE 13. I take a deep breath, my chest expands. *Symbol*: With the help of someone, I lift a table high."

"EXAMPLE 14. My blanket rests so heavily on one of my toes that it makes me nervous. *Symbol*: The top of a decorated canopied carriage scrapes against the branches of trees. A lady hits her hat against the top of the compartment."

"EXAMPLE 15. I have a rhinolaryngitis with a painful irritation which forces me to swallow saliva steadily. Fever. *Symbol*: Each time I am about to swallow I have a picture of a water bottle which I am supposed to swallow; after each swallow another takes its place" (p. 206).

Overall, Silberer offers numerous examples of each category, and also discusses the, at times, overlapping of the categories. His descriptions are vivid; his reasoning mostly compelling; and the cohesion of his arguments strong. Silberer is also clear to pay appropriate homage to Freud at the very onset of his exposition. Although he states that the psyche's capacity to engage in image-making activity occurs both in the hypnagogic state and in dreaming proper, he is careful to posit that the relationship between such is nonexistent. In other words, the autosymbolic phenomenon in the hypnagogic state does *not* correlate with the 'real' meaning of symbols in Freudian wish-fulfillment dream theory. At this early point in his theorizing, Silberer was cautious, noting that what he is discussing is an almost 'standalone' phenomenon, so as not to question the Freudian dream interpretation dogma of the time.

As an aside, what is also somewhat curious in this 1951 translation is the amount of footnoting the editor/translator engages in, and the extent to which clarifications are offered – as if the editor wants to be sure that Silberer does not make the reader stray from generally accepted Freudian doctrine.

Whatever the case, like a true scientist of old, Silberer clearly uncovered a phenomenon of significance, one which even impressed Freud, and which, to this day, is seen as a useful insight.

3   On symbol formation

Silberer's discussion on symbols was not as well received by Freud as that on the hypnagogic. In fact, probably quite telling in this regard in this second of Silberer's papers translated by Rapaport: "On Symbol-Formation" (pp. 208–233, Rapaport 1951) was the extensive footnoting throughout – even more extensive than in his paper on the hypnagogic. In fact, on certain pages of this work on symbols, the footnoting clarifications far exceeded Silberer's actual text. In addition, certain portions of the paper were (purposely?) omitted: e.g. Silberer's discussion of the teleological elements of psychoanalytic theory – hardly a neutral topic.

That being said, Silberer goes to great lengths in this paper to discuss the history and nature of symbols; to present their multidimensional nature; and to place them in context of the evolution of mankind. In so doing, his unique perspective on symbolism begins to emerge. For example, Silberer asserts: "This experience of sudden understanding, this feeling of close relatedness of meaning and symbol, is not specific to the application of psychoanalysis…" and adds "…Life is full of such symbols, and nobody can discover all of them. This is best illustrated by religious symbolism…" (p. 209).

Silberer does appropriately acknowledge major theorists of the time (e.g. Freud, Jung, Stekel, etc.) as he develops his position. He notes that psychoanalysts must routinely "…decipher symbols [that] must be considered the manifest expression of something latent…" (p. 208). He continues by saying that "…A symbol may remain uncomprehended for a long time; however, once it is interpreted, the enlightened observer will readily see the relatedness of the symbol and what it symbolizes…" and reminds the reader that "…a symbol may have several 'meanings'…" (p. 209). He adds, however, that such a pursuit is not the sole purview of psychoanalysis. In fact, it occurs "…wherever meaning-laden symbols are at first overlooked or misunderstood and then laboriously deciphered..." (p. 209). "Life is full of such symbols..." (p. 209), he proclaims, and reiterates that the best example of symbol-rich phenomena is religion.

Silberer also posits a central element of his understanding of symbols when he states that a symbol is "...an adequate form of 'the truth' for a given level of mental development..." (p. 209) – a level that can be compromised by various forms of intellectual or affective barriers. He then differentiates two types of symbols: *diluted* ("...the sign is arbitrarily chosen and could just as well be replaced by any other ... figure..." p. 210) and *essential* ("...a sign which has a close relationship to its meaning or meanings so that it cannot be changed without seriously interfering with this relationship..." p. 210) – with his focus of exploration clearly the latter.

As noted, such *essential* symbols are the stuff of psychoanalysis on an individual level, and in a parallel manner, of entire cultures on a mythological level. In fact, he eloquently observes that:

> modern ethnological and linguistic research contends that myths are not metaphoric expressions, allegory-like pictures deliberately invented by primitive people, but rather the only possible expression of their conception of nature, at the time, and for their mental development, adequate.
>
> (p. 212)

He continues that for such people, symbols are realities, except for "...a few exceptional individuals, ahead of their times..." (p. 212). Again, he notes that this group phenomena parallels the experience of the individual dreamer whose dream symbols seem real to him; or the "...compulsive neurotic [who] has no notion, unless apprised, that his obsessive ideas and compulsive actions are mere symbols..." (p. 213).

In a word: "...no one whose apperception is symbolic can at the time be clearly aware of the fact or of its extent..." (p. 213). This evolutionary notion of human consciousness means that "...later periods can see the symbolic and mythical in the conceptions of past periods..." (p. 214), and analogously on an individual level, the dreamer or neurotic can only grasp the true meaning of the symbolic if they are brought to a "...higher vantage-point..." (p. 214) by a skilled clinician.

Within this framework, Silberer then posits three more problems to explore: what is the *process* of symbol formation; what *conditions* bring it about; and what is its *purpose* (p. 213, emphasis added). As to 'process', he explains that the symbol is a hub of associations, that "... never hangs by a single thread, rather is part of the weave of a whole fabric..." (p. 214) and "...is said to have 'Praegnanz'..." (p. 215). He continues that the "...convergence of many association-chains in one point may be observed in myth-symbols of folk fantasy, as well as in symbols experienced by the individual ... known to psychoanalysis [as] *overdetermination* [or] *condensation*" (p. 215). In addition, symbol formation involves the human 'tendency to picturing': "...When a psychological entity undergoes symbolic substitution it takes on a sensory form, though otherwise it is more abstract..." (p. 216), which mirrors the Freudian notion of regression.

Furthermore, Silberer explains that there are essentially: "...two avenues open for the exploration of symbols..." (p. 216). The first is when "...the symbol appears as a substitution for something that I could under normal conditions clearly grasp [thus] the symbol appears when I am *no longer in command* of the idea underlying it..." (p. 216). He once again displays his evolutionary leanings when he describes the second mode: "If we now consider the developmental history of human knowledge, if we remember how, generation after generation, man pursues knowledge through series of images and mythologies – then the symbol appears as a substitute for ideas of which humanity has *no command as yet*...", or pointedly: "...If we follow the formation of symbols in the course of evolution, we find that they appear when man's mind reaches out for something which he cannot as yet grasp..." (pp. 216–217).

Silberer then offers a number of examples of the first option (i.e. 'no longer in command'), including his research on the auto-symbolic process noted in the previous chapter of this book on the hypnagogic phenomena, and adds that this illustrates "...the picturing process which produces symbols in its purest form and in strictest isolation from side issues..." (p. 218).

Silberer continues to discuss possible explanations of the conditions necessary to trigger the symbolizing process. Although the hypnogogic is clearly a by-product of fatigue, Silberer notes that there are other reasons why this shift from the cognitive demands of *apperceptive* thinking yield to the more primitive, pictorial *associative* thinking mode. He notes Jung's 'association experiments' and dream research as examples of how psychological 'complexes' that have 'multiply determined' symbols can cause apperceptive insufficiency, and default to the associative level. He adds that Freud pointed out the importance of *affective* interference, in compounding *apperceptive insufficiency*. Silberer concurs with Freud and expands the discussion to encompass "...a want of development (as in childhood and/or preliterates), or a temporary weakening ... due to general decrease in energy available for thinking (as in sleep)..." as well as the more Freudian "...intervention of affects which by pleasure-mechanism make the progress of the idea difficult...", or the Jungian "...divert attention-energy to the autonomous complexes..." (p. 228).

Silberer expands the notion even further when he posits that affects *not only* play an interfering, negative role in apperceptive function. They also have a *positive role* in that "...with the attention-energy they attract, they tend to make effective the complexes to which they maintain..." (p. 228). Therefore, "...Strictly speaking ... the affects are not disturbing but, rather, positive factors in symbols-formation ... [their] subject-matter ... is transformed into a symbol..." (p. 228).

He continues by defining two broad categories of symbols. The first comes about as a result of cognitive limitation, unaffected by affectively influenced complexes. The second is more affectively influenced: "... an idea is translated into a picture in a competitive struggle with other complexes. This amounts to a sidetracking of the idea as it strives toward consciousness..." (p. 229). He notes that in the first instance, "... though the idea striving to become conscious does not emerge in a clear form, it remains *undistorted* ... as though an object observed through a uniformly woven veil..." (p. 229). Meanwhile, in the second instance, the idea "...emerges unclear and displaced ... as though an object were observed through a spotted veil or through optically distorting glasses..." (p. 230). Silberer adds that both types have a certain 'subjective necessity', while the first type frequently also has an 'objective necessity' (i.e. the process "...yields symbols which appear valid and successful even to the outsider..." p. 230). He classifies most mythological symbols in this category. As to the second type, he overgeneralizes from his limited vantage point by stating: "...the intensity of the influence of the second type is most clearly seen in people of different racial (cultural) characteristics. In people who have the same characteristics, the rules of affect-interference are the same..." (p. 230). He then continues on this somewhat philosophical tact when he postulates that evolution involves periodic leaps from "...associative-perceptual to apperceptive-conceptual thinking..." (p. 231).

Silberer closes this discussion of symbolism and its meaning by proposing somewhat predictably that the ultimate *purpose* of symbol-formation might be: "...a finalistic (teleological) point of view, which is the counterpart of the causal point of view..." (p. 232) – i.e. the 'parsimonious' (cynical?) Freudian metaphysic of the time. In fact, his conclusion merits reproducing:

If the intelligence aspect of the psychic apparatus is rated by its useful function of gaining knowledge, then symbol-thinking certainly appears to be purposive. In the course of the development of intelligence, the mechanism of symbol-formation effects an understanding of that which is as yet not understandable. Thus are gathered the threads of knowledge out of which man weaves his concepts.

(p. 233)

Thus, Silberer's contribution to an understanding of symbolism and its meaning is robust. On a societal level, it honors their 'high value', multidetermined nature, as well as their essential, evolutionary role (via mythology) in the development of human consciousness. On an individual level, they likewise 'condense' multiple levels of meaning, including unconscious 'complexes' that are striving for attention.

The logical extension of such a deep appreciation of symbols is Silberer's interest in the mysterious realm of alchemy, and relatedly, his later immersion into Masonry, as well as his expansive vision of dreams and their meaning. Accordingly, we will now review some of his thoughts on the value and meaning of alchemy.

4 Alchemy
And problems of mysticism and its symbolism

If Silberer was skating on thin ice with Freudian orthodoxy with his delicate discussion of the hypnagogic, and perhaps on even thinner ice when exploring the genesis and purpose of symbols, the aforementioned *Problems of Mysticism and Its Symbolism* (written in 1914, and later renamed *Hidden Symbolism of Alchemy and the Occult Arts* (2015)) clearly landed him in a pond of apostacy from which he would never emerge.

Frankly, this is a learned and comprehensive book. Yet, like most works of that early period (when authors struggled for language to describe the newly fathomed unconscious), it is (as noted previously), at times, obtuse, confusing, and obscure. It also smacks of philosophical and religious idealism, almost implying that the true goal of all introspection, including psychoanalysis, is a level of self- awareness and self-development that aims for alignment with the universe and transcendence. Along such lines (also as noted earlier), it is repetitive and meditative in certain sections – and unabashedly spiritual. However, it is well supported, and almost encyclopedic in its inclusion of multiple references to religion, mythology, and the history of mankind.

As per Silberer's other writings, the work is logically structured, beginning with a lengthy parable from a sixteenth-century *Rosicrucian* text – a secret philosophical society founded in late medieval Germany. The parable is the hub of the book's remaining chapters. Silberer references and explores it from various theoretical perspectives, as if it were an epic dream, in his effort to delineate the attainment of the highest level of wisdom and self-awareness humanly possible.

Given its centrality in the work, a summary of the main dramatic elements of the parable is appropriate. Since it is lengthy and rambling, yet delineated into 21 distinct sections, I will likewise summarize it by section, and hopefully give the reader a sense of the world into which Silberer comfortably traversed. It proceeds as follows:

1. While walking through a forest and pondering life's existential miseries, the narrator wonders onto an 'untrodden path', and in spite of his desire to exit it, is pushed further along it by a powerful wind.
2. He adjusts and does not "...mind the rough walking..." (p. 7).
3. He then arrived at a 'meadow of felicity' where a group of mostly old, bearded men were discussing a host of subjects including the "...great and lofty mystery, hidden in Nature..." (p. 7) and revealed by God only to "...the few who loved him..." (p. 7).
4. After listening to this discussion for a while, the narrator could no longer contain himself, expressed and defended his opinions, and was eventually accepted by the group as one of its members.
5. However, the group makes it clear that he could not be fully accepted as a colleague unless the narrator gets to know their lion, and his powers and abilities, and then *subdues* him (i.e. the lion).
6. The narrator entered the lion's den, is terrified by its ferociousness, tries in vain to caress him, and then utilizes his (the narrator's) athletic acumen to subdue him. In the process, he "...forced the blood out of his body, yea, even out of his heart ... [the blood] was beautifully red but very choleric [and] his bones were white as snow..." (p. 8).
7. Upon reviewing the narrator's feat, the elders decided that he needed to bring the lion back to life. The narrator refused and in his escape wound up on a very high and narrow wall with a man "... several paces before me..." (p. 8).
8. As the narrator tried to descend the wall, it was unclear which was the safest route to take, but he eventually "...risked it, trusted to my good feet, held myself tight, and came down without harm..." (p. 9).
9. The narrator then arrived at a great, walled-in rose garden enclosing a host of young men and young women slowly working both in pairs, and on their own at the same time. The narrator notes that "...their work was familiar to me..." and was also "...dirty and sloppy..." (p. 9).
10. As he approached the gate to get in, the narrator received resentful gazes from those who had labored outside the garden extensively but were never allowed in. The narrator, however, quite deftly gains entry into the garden and gains access to other unlocked doors in the garden.
11. When in the garden, the narrator meets a young couple on their way "...out of this beautiful garden into our apartment to enjoy the pleasures of love..." (p. 10). He also saw a large mill with several water wheels that was inexplicably unable to grind. The narrator then encounters the band of elders again that make it known that if

the couple consummates their marriage "...the lion will then regain his life and become more powerful and mighty than before..." (p. 11)

12. The narrator was relieved and pleased that the couple would fulfill what the elders had prescribed.

13. The narrator then observes that the bridegroom is wearing "... brilliant scarlet clothes..."; the bride a "...white satin coat..."; and the bridegroom's mother was "...still so young she appeared to be just born..." (p. 11)

14. Things then take a horrible turn. It is revealed that the couple are brother and sister, and are to be punished by being locked naked in a stark, transparent chamber for all to see – and the narrator is given the charge of guarding the couple to ensure they remain imprisoned. Matters grow worse when the narrator tries to warm the couple's chamber by starting a small fire. The warmth from the fire causes the couple to passionately embrace, the young man literally melts away in his lover's arms, and she in turn cries herself to death – flooding the chamber with her tears. As the narrator notes: "... Ah woe is me. In what pain, and need and trouble was I that my two charges had quite disappeared in water, and death alone was left for me..." (p. 12).

15. In his despair, the narrator reflects upon "...how Medea had revived the dead body of Aeson..." (p. 12), and begins in earnest a prolonged process (i.e. "...forty whole days...") of slowly evaporating the water in the flooded chamber via a small and steady fire. Over time, the "...corpses ... black as coal, began again to be visible ... dead and rotten ... hideously stinking..." (p. 12). The narrator also observes a daily pattern of the water evaporating; a small cloud forming; and then a "...very fruitful dew, which very early in the morning fell and moistened the earth and washed our dead corpses..." (p. 13), which slowly seemed to bring them back to life. He also notes that given the fact the chamber was hermetically sealed, the souls and the spirits of these lovers were still inside of it. The first to rise was the young woman, the "...transfigured body of the queen..." (p. 13).

16. This queen proclaims that "after having been humbled, I am a queen elevated over many kingdoms. I have been killed and made to live..." (p. 13).

17. She also notes that although her brother has yet to rise, he will be more powerful than her when he does.

18. The narrator then witnesses invisible tailors preparing the finest of clothing (e.g. "...a red velvet garment with precious rubies...", p. 13) for the 'soon to rise' king.

19. As expected, "...the great and mighty king appeared in great splendor and magnificence..." (p. 13), and "...begged me [the narrator] with (such) friendly and gracious words..." (p. 13) that he (the narrator) gladly disobeyed his orders, and released him from the chamber.
20. After "...pass[ing] the dog days in great heat..." (p. 14), the king returned to the chamber, asked the narrator to fetch him water specifically from the aforementioned mill to further restore his health, and then went to sleep.
21. The narrator then recounts glowingly that after a few days of sleep, and after having his fill of the "...lordly and wholesome water..." (p. 14), the king emerged; and his appearance was so impressive the narrator states that "...I never saw a more lordly person nor more lordly demeanor..." (p. 14). The king then proceeds to let the narrator into his chamber, and remarkably shares the secrets of the ages with him. Specifically, the narrator reports "...there was no end of gold or carbuncle there; rejuvenation and restoration of natural forces, and also recovery of lost health, and removal of all diseases were a common thing in that place..." (p. 14). He continues that "...The most precious of all was that the people of that land knew their creator, feared and honored him, and asked of him wisdom and understanding..." (p. 14)

Quite a striking way to begin a potentially psychoanalytically informed book, especially at a time when Freud was rigorously aspiring to create a pure (secular) science! It also illustrates Silberer's interest in the mystical, the mythological, and the historical; as well as his aforementioned writing style of meshing his theoretical positions with lengthy, colorful narratives. As will also become abundantly clear, the parable teems with alchemical themes that ground later Masonic thought, and is wholly consistent with Silberer's expansive, and historically and theologically informed, understanding of symbolism.

However, because Silberer clearly aspired to 'belong' to the psychoanalytic community, especially so early in his brief career, he ambitiously attempted to integrate the various strands of psychoanalytic, alchemical, and Masonic thought in the work. Accordingly, he devoted the first chapter to an appraisal of the parable from the psychoanalytic perspective. This appraisal will be discussed later in this book. As will be seen, Silberer goes to great lengths to try to find the drive-derivative, latent meaning in almost every symbol and action of the story. True to form, however, he sprinkles such with references from literature, religion, and mythology – which certainly dilutes his effort to approximate dogmatic Freudian orthodoxy.

The next chapter of this early defining work focuses on alchemy – a field that he believed held great potential in understanding the human psyche, and as such could contribute markedly to the newly minted insights of psychoanalysis. In fact, Jung has famously noted that: "Herbert Silberer has the merit of being the first to discover the secret threads that lead from alchemy to the psychology of the unconscious" (Jung 1955–1957, p. 792).

Accordingly, Silberer begins his exploration by offering a historical overview of alchemy, making note that this method of "...gold mining and extraction, were guarded as a royal secret..." (p. 56) in Egypt, its country of origin. Once again reflecting his evolutionary focus, he notes that this primitive notion of making gold from other elements was an understandable aspiration of people of their time given "...the phase in the development of human thought..." (p. 56) they inhabited. He goes on to discuss Paracelsus innovation involving the combination of mercury, sulphur, and salt in the pursuit of this elusive precious substance. He also highlights the fact the early alchemists (i.e. Babylonians) attempted to match metals with the planets as they were understood at the time: Saturn/lead; Jupiter/tin; Mars/iron; Venus/copper; Mercury/quicksilver; and even the Sun/gold; and the Moon/silver.

Silberer continues that during "...the most flourishing period of alchemy ... In spite of the diversity of the representations we find certain fundamental principles which are in general firmly established..." (p. 60). These principles include: "...interaction or the cooperation of two things that are generally called man and woman, red and white, sun and moon, sulphur and mercury..."; and "...we must derive a male activity from the gold, and a female from the silver..." (p. 60). In addition, stones must be melted to their original 'prima material' (i.e. their purest form); and such prima material needed to be washed as well as subjected to a putrefaction process in order to achieve this lofty goal.

From this alchemical vantage point, Silberer then explores the aforementioned parable in his search for what he calls the "...alchemic hieroglyphics..." (p. 62). To begin, he notes that, among other things, the wanderer is searching for truth, and as per the hermetic tradition, the elders are ambivalent in their communications about it. Also, as to the wanderer's slaying of the lion, he notes "...The wanderer kills the lion and takes out of him red blood and white bones, therefore red and white, Red and white enter later as roses; then as man and woman..." (p. 62). He continues that the workers who are slovenly parallel the reputation of the alchemists who are oftentimes critiqued as "...'bunglers' and 'messy cooks'..." (p. 64). The garden is a 'rose garden' frequently referenced by the alchemists. The locking and unlocking of doors in the parable suggests the alchemists' efforts to bind and unbind chemical combinations in search of their desired metal. The mill reflects the alchemists' efforts of fermentation, and their use of metals in the process.

Silberer continues: "...Now begins the main work – marriage, prison, embrace, conception, birth, transfiguration..." (p. 65), and references numerous sources to illustrate parallels to such themes. For example, the sealed chamber is seen as the proverbial 'philosophical egg', the womb, or the kiln – protected enclosures where life can emerge. Life emerges only after death and putrefaction, in which spirit somehow fuses in this rebirth process. Like the alchemists' pursuit of the proper hues and mixtures, the reborn lovers emerge with radiant garments of striking blends of colors. Additionally, the daily cycle of the life-giving dew that restores the health of the lovers suggests the alchemists' notion of the essential 'elixir of life'. Also, the fundamental concept of the regeneration contained in the parable (i.e. creating the animate from the inanimate) is at the core of the alchemists' pursuit. Silberer also notes that it is the central impetus for the pursuit of the homunculus (to be discussed separately in the next chapter of this book).

Silberer then goes on to elaborate on what he clearly considers the underlying, very lofty aims of the alchemical process – crediting Ethan Allen Hitchcock (*Remarks upon Alchemy and the Alchemists*, 1857) throughout the discussion. Silberer asserts: "...Any one that makes a thorough assessment of the alchemistic literature must be struck with the religious seriousness that prevails..." and "...even in their beginnings, alchemistic theories were blended with cosmogonic and religious ideas ... something more ... than a mere chemical recipe..." (p. 71). He continues: "...It should, however, not be surprising to us who are acquainted with the philosophical presuppositions of alchemy, that in addition to the chemical and mechanical side of alchemy, a philosophical and religious side also received consideration and care..." (p. 72). Given such, the ultimate gold to be created is mankind: i.e. "...Hitchcock with a single word furnishes us the key to the understanding of the hermetic masters when he says: The subject is man..." (p. 73). Silberer then unabashedly proceeds to make multiple religious, mostly Christian, references, that address the 'perfection' of mankind, the centrality of conscience (the true 'mercury'), and the interconnectedness of all men. He notes that "...the hermetic philosophers do not pursue speculative theology, but [rather, the] work of mysticism..." (p. 79). In his scholarly surveying, he also points out that much of eastern philosophy (e.g. Samkhya and Yoga) share such metaphysical emphases.

Silberer further explains that over the centuries, the alchemists, in order to avoid persecution from the "...narrow-minded church ... veiled their teachings..." (p. 81). In fact, referencing Hitchcock and endorsing the notion of the evolution of human consciousness, he states that the alchemists appeared to believe "...that the knowledge of their secret is (was) dangerous (for the generality of people) [and] the time was ripe for a religion that was based more on ideal requirements, on moral freedom, than on fear of hell fire, [and] expectation of rewards..." (p. 81).

Clearly so enthusiastically and scholarly an exposition of alchemy reflects Silberer' belief that it embodied some of the highest aspirations of mankind at its particular moment in the history of the evolution of human consciousness. It seems that he genuinely thought that an in-depth grasp of such writings and goals would be enlighteningly compatible with, and possibly an enhancement of, emerging psychoanalytic thought. It is unfortunately quite clear that such an effort, compounded by his obscure, rambling presentation, did not succeed with his psychoanalytic peers – especially at that time.

In spite of this, however, not only did Silberer speak highly of the alchemical pursuits of the previous centuries, but he made it quite clear that Freemasonry (note that he was a Mason, himself) was the natural outgrowth of alchemy, and embodied its highest goals and loftiest ideals. Accordingly, we will look more closely at his appreciation of the 'Royal Art' of Freemasonry in a later chapter of this book. However, before leaving our discussion of alchemy and its pursuit of perfection (i.e. purity of substance = perfection of the human 'spirit'), a separate discussion will focus on what was perceived as the alchemists' most ambitious pursuit: the scientific (i.e. alchemical) creation of human life in the form of the *homunculus* – as we review Silberer's early writing on the subject entitled *Der Homunculus* (1914).

5   The homunculus

Silberer's direct exploration of the alchemists' notion of the homunculus is telling on two levels. First, it further illustrates his belief in the importance of understanding alchemy, even to the point of closely assessing one of its most ambitious (and outrageous?) goals: creating a miniature human being in a scientific laboratory. Second, it favorably reflects on how open-minded and curious a thinker Silberer actually was: going to great lengths to research and explain this obscure phenomenon and its implicit symbolic meaning. Again, it probably also illustrates once again his hope that this would be a positive contribution to the developing field of psychoanalysis, with its goal of understanding the nature of man. Accordingly, we join Silberer's discussion of the matter, as well as his telling of a delightful, almost mythological, tale as part of it.

In the beginning of *Der Homunculus*, Silberer sets the stage with a quote from Goethe's *Faust* in which Wagner whispers: "A Man is being made" (p. 1). Silberer situates this uncanny pursuit in the world of alchemy, and notes that alchemy is "…interfused with concepts related to procreation…" (p. 1). He refers the reader to his *Problems of Mysticism and Its Symbolism* (discussed in the previous chapter of this book) for a more thorough exploration of what he calls 'this venerable art'. He notes that alchemy also addresses other impulses (e.g. the Oedipal drama), but has a particularly keen emphasis on *improvement* (i.e. "…this art of 'improving' metals … the establishment of a new order … a new, improved creation or form of creation…" (p. 3). He further observes that there are a "…great number of infantile (or, if you will, primitive) theories that, like mythological and alchemical imagery, feature notions of procreation…" (p. 3).

Silberer then goes on to describe common themes in these procreation theories. One is the consistent notion of **putrefaction**, the essentially "…spermatic quality of excretions (excrement, urine, etc.)…"

(p. 4). Germination and growth can occur only after decay. On a parallel spiritual track, (e.g. John 24:12), new life can only emerge if death occurs. This putrefaction is also known as 'blackening', and in certain myths is associated with the black raven.

A second common theme is that of **dismemberment**: i.e. the decaying material needs to be 'broken up'. Once so atomized, this raw material is ideally placed in a warm, moist container – sometimes called 'the philosopher's egg' – for nine months to reconstitute. Silberer notes that Rank has written extensively on this "...primitive and infantile procreation theory..." involving "...the generation of a new being from dismembered parts..." (p. 4). Also, related to the above-noted 'moist container' is the obvious amniotic fluid, and in more mythical renderings, tales of great floods, or infants in baskets rescued in rivers, etc. Relatedly, the 'basket' parallels Noah's Ark, and from a psychoanalytic perspective, such "...containers ... are the psychological expression of the maternal womb..." (p. 6).

Silberer returns to his initial observation when he essentially concurs with C. G. Jung that "...procreation themes are so heavily interwoven in the goals of alchemical work that it must come as no surprise that they have at times detached themselves from the rest and gained some degree of independence..." (pp. 7–8). He does note, however, that there were ancient writers who touched upon the notion of creation, and in fact, asserts that it was Paracelsus (late fifteenth and first half of the sixteenth century) who actually offered instructions on how to create the homunculus.

Silberer then proceeds to generously quote significant portions of Paracelsus' work. Such is striking for its matter-of-fact stance toward man's clear capacity to create life from putrefaction or in sealed, moist, glass containers, be it birds, small animals, insects, or even the infamous *basilisk* monster (the sight of which alone could be deadly). As noted above, themes of decay, moist enclosure, and regeneration of dismembered components appear to be central in such creation pursuits.

From such a vantage point, Paracelsus offers the following guidance in creating a homunculus. First, mix semen of a man with horse manure and place it in the stomach of a horse for 40 days, or until it begins to move. At this juncture, it should resemble a human being, though it will be transparent. It should now be fed daily with the Arcanum of human blood, and allowed to thrive in the nurturing atmosphere of the horse's stomach. At the end of this period, it will resemble a human infant, yet be much smaller, and will be known a homunculus. Such a being should initially be educated, but once mature will have no need for further education. In fact, homunculi will possess extraordinary intellectual ability; be very capable of teaching others; and in fact, be themselves capable of producing other unusual creatures including pygmies and giants. Silberer then notes that there are many examples in mythology that illustrate "…that seed that doesn't germinate in a natural way may produce monstrous beings, particularly ones with superhuman abilities…" (p. 15).

Silberer continues to offer examples of palingenesis in folklore and mythology. Examples range from the production of a rose from its ashes; the creation of a crab from its deconstructed parts; "…use[ing] the ashes of the decomposing child corpse to make the image of that child appear in a glass vessel…"; and "…in an African myth, a barren woman extracts a drop of blood, puts it in a pot for nine months, and then finds a baby inside…" (p. 17).

He then shifts to some of the 'darker' sides of the homunculus pursuit, and the work of the alchemists in general. He quotes Paracelsus' detailed warning of the monstrous outcomes and creatures that result from the wanton behavior of sodomites. Silberer also reports on the fraudulent, criminal activities of a late eighteenth-century Viennese alchemical society that pursued 'star mucus' or 'star slime' supposedly captured from shooting stars in the belief that such substance would be a 'prima materia' – from which gold could be produced, and the homunculus could be created. He adds that upon prosecution, it became known that many of the group were "…stercorists, seminalists, and sanguinists…" (p. 21) who not only gathered the urine, sperm, and feces of volunteers for their alchemical pursuits, but also drained blood from such participants. He also cites the tragic story of one of the victims of this group: "…a young woman was found dying … as a result of the blood loss she had sustained in just one hour from the veins opened on her hands and feet…" (p. 22) – clearly underscoring the dangers of so grandiose a pursuit.

To further expand his discussion, Silberer explores related themes at length, including the common notion of a 'spirit in a bottle', which is oftentimes seen as malevolent (demonic), yet nevertheless prescient and extremely perceptive. He then notably detours into a related construct in the homunculus *genre*: "…the phenomenon associated with the *Alraun*, or the mandrake root [which] in its day … was known as a homunculus…" (p. 26).

Silberer explains that the mandrake was a "…human-shaped magical root which one would keep safe and which one expected to exercise a luck-bringing influence on one's affairs…" and was actually "…regarded as an entity with a personality…" (p. 26). The legend of its conception is as follows: "…When a notorious thief who is still a youth is hanged, and urine or semen falls to the ground, there will grow under the gallows tree a broad-leaved, yellow-blossomed mandrake plant..." (p. 27). Silberer goes on to detail the many steps required to actually secure the plant (including essentially sacrificing a dog's life), since the mandrake's shrill screams are so caustic they are deadly. However, once the mandrake is secured: "...the root is lifted out, washed in red wine, wrapped in white and red silk, placed in a small box, bathed every Friday, at every new moon, and wrapped in a fresh white 'undershirt'..." (p. 27).

In addition to its propitious properties, the mandrake was rumored to: serve as an aphrodisiac; enhance women's fertility; induce drowsiness; and function as an anesthetic in surgery. Silberer notes that its alleged magical powers troubled the religious community, as did its resemblance to male genitalia – rendering it somewhat of a 'phallic amulet'. He relates an instance where: "...a Franciscan monk in 1429 ... gave a forceful sermon against the mandrake amulet [and] convinced the attending men and women of its uselessness and had several roots handed over and burnt..." (p. 29). Yet, as a counterpoint, Silberer shares a letter written from one brother to another: the former very concerned about the consistent misfortunes of the latter. The concerned brother earnestly states: "...your misfortune comes not from God, but from people full of malice, and nothing can be done about your situation *unless you acquire a mandrake...*" (p. 30, emphasis added).

In the final section of this paper on the homunculus, Silberer shares a fascinating, 'fairy tale' like story recounted in an ancient book entitled *The Sphinx*. In it, a Freemason servant named Josef Kammerer details the adventures of his superior, the mid-eighteenth-century Austrian Count Kueffstein (a Masonic Worshipful Master) and his clergyman companion, Abbe Geloni. Apparently, during their travels in Italy, their common Free Masonry and Rosicrucian beliefs drew them together and they "...would hold long discussions about the secret sciences that would go on all day and all night, foregoing food, drink, and sleep..." (p. 36).

A key focus of such talks was the possibility of creating a homunculus. In apparent pursuit of such, they chose to spend "...a period of nine weeks ... in a certain Carmelite monastery deep in the mountains, where the monks received them with great demonstrations of respect and hospitality..." (p. 36). During a five-week period of this stay, Kueffstein and Geloni utilized the monastery's "...excellently equipped laboratory..." (p. 36) to "...labour day and night ... the fire was never allowed to go out [and] *actually did succeed in creating ten spirits* ... a King, a Queen, a Knight, a Monk, a Mason, a Miner, a Seraph, a Nun, and finally a blue and red spirit..." (p. 36, emphasis added).

These spirits were then individually sealed into glass jars partially filled with water and buried for four weeks in a pile of manure to enable them to grow – analogous to the alchemists' notion of putrefaction in the making of gold. The experiment was a success: "…the 'things' had grown 'each almost one and a half spans long', so that their glass containers had become almost too small for them…" (p. 38). Abbe Geloni then "…dressed each of the eight spirits according to its standing and rank … so that they were all very nicely attired…" (p. 38). The blue and red spirits were not as easily contained: "…The face of the blue ghost was quite kind and saintly … the face of the red spirit was however 'white as a sheet', impertinent and nasty, like that of a malevolent demon…" (p. 39).

Count Kueffstein proceeded to bring the ten homunculi home to his native Austria, and care for them in multiply complex and ritualistic ways. According to Kammerer, the homunculi were engaged in "…experiments … [involving] soothsaying … magical sessions [and] 'when the mood took them', they deigned to favour the astonished brothers … in revelations of the most wondrous kind and prophesies that 'almost always' came true…" (p. 41). Conversely, however, "In a bad mood, they were of course exceedingly 'contrary and intractable'" (p. 41), which clearly strained the patience and good humor of the Count. In fact, what became of these unique creatures is unclear, although a note from 1781 reflects the Count stating that he had "… long ago 'rid himself of them' and wished to hear no more about these 'little devils', for both his wife and his father confessor had repeatedly urged him not to jeopardise his salvation with such blasphemous tomfoolery…" (p. 43).

Silberer then proceeds to sum up why he so extensively explored this homunculus phenomenon. He points out that he in no way endorses the authenticity of this "…raucous 'homunculiad' … originat[ing] in the wild flight of fancy of one or, quite likely, more persons … perhaps sparked by the addle-brained misunderstanding of some actual experiments, and populated with undigested alchemical-magical elements…" (p. 43). Rather, what he finds of note is the parallel between the underlying themes as well as motives of the homunculus story with those of creation myths over the ages, and on a deeper level the effort of psychoanalysis to discover "…psychical *Urmotive* as the prime movers…" (p. 44).

Silberer then sketches out some of these basic parallels; for example: "…glass vessels … filled with water … corresponds to the 'philosopher's egg' … and the 'flood motif' … a mythological expression of procreation and birth in the service of myth-forming tendencies…"

(p. 44). Similarly: "...the homunculi are baked ... 'Baking' is a well-known image symbolizing the gestation of an infant ... the alchemical 'infant' needs nine months to ripen inside the philosopher's egg ... the spirits need nine weeks to be ready..." (p. 44). Or "...the water in the glass jars – the water that the spirits need to live – corresponds on the one hand to that mythical water (of life and of death) ... and in a narrower interpretation, to the amniotic fluid..." (pp. 44–45). Additionally, he compares the various processes of impregnation to begin creation, as well as the similarities between "...the blood used to nourish the spirits [and] intrauterine nutrition..." (p. 45). He hypothesizes from a psychoanalytic stance that the "...magical-hermetical seal for the jars..." is "...a proscription or inhibition against some forbidden act ... of unnatural procreation [and] relate to incest..." (p. 45). He also once again mentions the obvious phallic quality of the mandrake as well as the homunculus.

Silberer asserts his hope that he has "...sufficiently demonstrated ... my [his] initial claim – that alchemical symbolism fits well at numerous points into the system of 'folk-psychological parallels to infantile sexual theories' – *is true also of the particular idea of the creation of the homunculus...*" (p. 46, emphasis added). He then makes two final points – somewhat characteristic of the different theoretical worlds he attempts to merge. In allegiance to the nascent psychoanalytic theory of the time, he links the unnatural creation of the homunculi and the consequent atypical results with the Freudian notion of an "...'overevaluation' of onanism..." (p. 46), and the frequent psychoanalytic exploration of masturbation as well as incest. On the other hand, and true to his experience as a balloonist, he finds a second core motive in the homunculus story to be the uniquely human desire for "...improvement – specifically, the one of improved creation or procreation..." (p. 48). He closes with a quote from *Faust* that proclaims that "...we, as Men, with all our greater gifts, begin, to have, as we should, a nobler origin..." (p. 48).

Thus, Silberer, once again, especially in his earlier works, clearly attempted to mesh the worlds of mythology, mysticism, and alchemy with that of emerging psychoanalysis.

However, one sees a less ambitious effort to merge such worlds in his discussion of the value of Freemasonry and its symbols – presented in the following chapter. Possibly because this represents some of his later work, the eagerness to 'fit in' with doctrinaire psychoanalysis may have been less pressing, and the criticism he had apparently received, somewhat jading. Whatever the case, these lectures reflect an overall focused and lucid stance, and deserve notice from a number of vantage points including the historical.

6 Masonic writings

As noted, once Silberer attempted to translate the sixteenth-century Rosicrucian parable in *Problems of Mysticism and Its Symbolism* from a psychoanalytic and then alchemical stance, he proceeded to discuss what many believe was a logical outgrowth of alchemy, and Rosicrucianism: Freemasonry. He observed that the Rosicrucians were a secret philosophical psychology founded in late medieval Germany that developed in a piecemeal, disjointed fashion, and eventually transformed into a emerging Freemasonry movement. He explains: "...Freemasonry must have felt some affinity with Rosicrucianism, something related at the psychical basis of the mode of expression (symbolism, ritual) of both..." (p. 96). He continues that in its purest form Rosicrucianism was "...identical with the higher alchemy..." yet when misconstrued could "...incite weaker characters to a perverted idea and practice of it..." (p. 96). Silberer clearly believed that Freemasonry was above such degenerate behavior, and to the contrary served to inspire what he called "the seeker". Specifically, he proclaims: "...What impels the seeker, that is, the man who actually serves the name, in masonry and in alchemy, is clearly manifested as a certain dissatisfaction ... he expects more, wants to have more exhaustive information, wants to know when the "real" will be finally shown..." (p. 97). Masonry – and Rosicrucianism and alchemy before it – if practiced appropriately, attempts to "...remove the erroneous opinion from them (i.e. the disciples) in so far as they are infected with it, even on the first step of the temple of wisdom..." (p. 98). Accordingly, Silberer saw unlimited possibility in the alchemical/Masonic world – so much so that he became a Mason himself.

Such affection for Masonry was nowhere more clearly evident than in the series of four lectures he delivered before the Grand Lodge of Vienna beginning on November 30, 1919 (published in the first edition of *Psyche and Eros* [July 1920, Vol. 1, No. 1, pp. 17–24]). In these lectures, Silberer continues and expands upon his earlier discussed theory of the nature of symbols, and in so doing, comprehensively explores the rich symbolic tradition of Freemasonry. All four lectures were published in *Psyche and Eros* between 1920 and 1921. As noted, they reflect Silberer's mature, and frequently compelling, thinking, and are worthy of review. In addition, they are historically educational, and once again reflect Silberer's scholarly, intellectually curious disposition.

To begin, in the initial portion of the first lecture, Silberer discloses Kantian leanings when he notes that Kant's theory of the 'categories' reflects the philosopher's effort to make sense out of the "...infinite variety of phenomena..." by attempting to uncover "...a system of principles by which the universe might be explained: abbreviations in the book of nature..." (p. 17). He then offers an overview of the history of such efforts over the centuries, including: the astrological categories of the Babylonians and the Chaldeans; the ideograms and alphabet of the Jewish 'Cabala'; the Pythagorean doctrine of numbers; the elevated, somewhat spiritual realm of ideas of Plato; and Kant's forerunner, Aristotle's categories. From this vantage point, he asserts that Freemasonry not only shares a relationship and affinity with such systems of symbols, but in fact has "...even retained much of their matter, something from each – and there was something good in all of them..." (p. 18).

In this preliminary discussion, Silberer makes another interesting point (which he embellishes on at other junctures in his work): as systems of framing reality become outmoded (e.g. laws of astrology), they do not completely disappear, but rather "...their mortal remains become the heritage of *superstition*..." (p. 18, emphasis added). He astutely adds that such outdated world views were "...a necessary step in man's advance..." and admonishes the reader: "...let us not be so naïve as to think that later generations, thousands of years hence, may not find our mode of looking at the world childish..." (p. 19).

So what, then, is a symbol? Silberer is clear to differentiate a symbol from what he calls the "...thin, dry ... conventional and vapid..." (p. 19) *allegorical picture* (e.g. Neptune with his crown and trident representing sovereignty of the seas; woman with a mural crown as a representation of a city; etc.). Such representations are almost one dimensional, and can almost be described as if they were a mathematical equation.

Symbols, on the other hand, are "...much more pregnant..." and are "...teeming with meaning..." (p. 19). They are "...the points of intersection where many lines of thought meet [or] like suns from which rays of significance emanate...", and are "...distinguished by a more intimate connection with the thing it represents..." (p. 19). Silberer references the work of Freidrich Creuzer as he discusses symbols over the ages; he (Silberer) states that a symbol involves an 'encounter' with an idea, including its 'hidden' meanings, and is actually the "...sensible, concrete embodiment of the idea itself..." (p. 20).

Silberer furthermore maintains that symbols need to meet certain 'requirements': i.e. paradoxically, clarity and brevity. Symbols need to carry multiple meanings and implications, yet do so dynamically, rapidly, and efficiently. And as to the 'origins' of such potent phenomena – particularly many of those embedded in Freemasonry – Silberer provides an evolutionary perspective that accounts for the cognitive state and limitations of mankind in a particular era. The lynchpin of his thesis is what he calls 'capacity': the ability of a given person (or peoples) to fully comprehend a construct or idea at his (their) point in time. As he initially proposed in his earlier paper on symbol formation, he noted that if such 'capacity' is unable to grasp this idea, the concept is converted imagistically into the 'symbol' – which becomes the 'pregnant' shorthand for the unintelligible and/or inexpressible thought. Thus, for primitive societies up until our present age, symbols serve to express thoughts that cannot be adequately understood at the time.

Silberer's support of this thesis is familiar: he presents two clinical examples from his work on the hypnagogic phenomena, and his related explorations of dreams (both discussed in more detail in other sections of this text). In the first example, as he attempts to wrestle with some of the interpersonal crises embroiled in Goethe's *Faust* (a performance of which he had seen earlier that evening), his abstract thoughts 'break down' and are replaced with very vivid images (e.g. a rocky jetty by a dark sea with a dim horizon in the distance) that *symbolically* represent the complex thoughts that he is unable to maintain due to his fatigue. Similarly, in the second example, again in which his fatigue means he is unable to sustain concentration on a fairly complex interpersonal dilemma, such concepts convert to rich, fluid *symbols*, the analysis of which reflects a myriad of meanings directly pertinent to the aforementioned dilemma. Thus, like entire populations transforming inexplicable thoughts to symbols, individuals, cognitively unable to keep focus on concepts due to fatigue, experience the automatic conversion of such into teeming symbols that carry the many elements of the thoughts.

Silberer summarizes his position in this first lecture poetically by observing "...just as ideas 'dawn' in our personal experience, so do they 'dawn' with even greater richness of image, in the slow evolution of the ethnic mind, of humanity. The dawning great idea does not announce itself in the abstract forms that mark mental mastery, but in symbols – in pledges of its presence..." (p. 23).

He adds a few more reflections from Creuzer depicting a spiritual element of symbolism: i.e. the 'soul' *striving for expression* (i.e. "Painful is the longing to give birth to the infinite in the finite…") (p. 23). Silberer concludes by once again commending his audience by asserting:

…We may, then, conceive the symbol as a full cup of promise, filled at first with a turgid, then with an ever purer drink – invigorating poison from celestial streams. Such is the highest type of symbol. And freemasonry is rich in images of this sort.

(p. 24)

Silberer's second lecture entitled "II. The Symbolism of Building" (*Psyche and Eros*, Vol I, No. 2, Sept.–Oct. 1920) hones in on the rich, complex, and multidimensional history of Freemasonry in Austria as well as Europe in general. He notes that although Freemasonry in Austria was "enabled to resume overt activity only with the birth of the Republic in the fall of 1918…" (p. 84), it had existed for centuries in various covert lodges and gathering places. He observes that its connection with the building trade is somewhat enigmatic, yet seems to correspond to the global German term 'Steinmetzen' (stone mason) – an outgrowth of the highly skilled craftsmen, sculptors, and architects who designed, built, and decorated the grand cathedrals of the Middle Ages. Over the years, he adds that the ideals of masonry expanded beyond the building trade, and began to incorporate more intangible, somewhat spiritual, aspirations. Silberer explains this phenomenon: "… The fact that liberal thought – always menaced, and cruelly menaced, by the ungenerous powers of the state – happened to find shelter and encouragement among the builders (even if not among the builders exclusively) is explicable on several grounds…" (p. 86). Such grounds included the fact that stone mason organizations were widespread yet tended to have rigidly maintained membership; valued and maintained certain age-old traditions; and fostered free, artistic expression – similar to the societies of artists during the Renaissance.

Silberer credits Dr. Ludwig Keller for his in-depth look at Masonic history. Of particular note was the extreme effort groups went to in order to keep their membership, practices, and special knowledge base secret. In fact, "Among the secrets of master masons belonged the appropriate building plan ('gerechter Steinmetzengrund'), that is, the basic rules governing the technique of construction…" (p. 87). Also impressive among the Masonic lodges, unlike other guilds or societies, was the universal notion of equality and brotherhood. Although there were demarcated roles and responsibilities, all members of the lodge saw each other as brothers.

The demarcation of such roles and their literal reflection of the design of the actual construction of such lodges is Silberer's entry point to illustrate the extensive, embedded use of symbolism in Freemasonry. For example, he explains:

> ...The lodge itself was in the shape of a longish rectangle, the narrow sides facing west and east. The master's seat was in the eastern end, the seats of the speaker and the wardens in the western, those of the master masons ('sodales') along the southern side, and along the northern were ranged the places of those of lowest degree – the travelling apprentices...
>
> (pp. 87–88)

He continues that the symbols used in the lodge and its rituals were derived from a host of sources: mathematics including geometry; nature; the building trade itself; and even Scripture. Such symbols had typically at least three levels of significance: the intellectual or ethical; the ethno-religious; and the vocational. To illustrate, Silberer asserts that "...the circle represents ethically the Divine Perfection, ritually the solidarity of the brotherhood, vocationally both the inherent structural principle and the office of the Master..." (p. 88), and again via the notion of 'condensation', so much more. He further states that over time, the craft of building expanded into the actual art of living life (i.e. "...that broader 'art' of the spirit which even to-day freemasonry calls the 'royal art' that is, as Weltanschauung (philosophy of life) and its ethical application...", p. 89).

Silberer notes that over the ages, from the secret societies of the catacombs to the guilds of the Renaissance to the lodges throughout Europe, the need to meet covertly, resist governmental and/or institutional religious control, and safeguard the life of the spirit, seems to have been served by such secret societies – along with their reliance on, and immersion into, universal symbols. He places Freemasonry in the position of both participant as well as inheritor of such activity, and thus a fertile place to explore this panoply of symbols. As he sees it, Freemasonry, maybe even more so than other of these societies, developed over the centuries because it had the need to keep its members protected; had the capacity to literally 'build' a structure to safeguard such, while simultaneously reflecting the myriad of 'multidetermined' symbols embedded in this group's values, procedures, and goals; and had the willingness and vision to perceive extensive parallels between the actual edifices it constructed and the human person whose body is the 'dwelling place' of its spiritual aspirations.

Again, Silberer concludes this second lecture elegantly by stating:

> ...There remains to be emphasized merely the thought that the organization of an enduring ethical association intended to shut out the noisy marketplace of the trivial everyday life – an association which must inevitably be thought of as an asylum and a house for the better self – an undertaking such as this presents many analogies to the building of a house; and it must be further remembered that any striving that is accompanied by strong feelings and intense longing seldom fails, as soon as it speaks in images, to represent itself, too, in these symbols with the help of a functional symbolism, that is, to an objective representation of the philosophical ideas there will then be spontaneously conjoined a representation of the striving toward the glimpsed ideals...
>
> (pp. 96–97)

He also sets the stage for his next lecture by reminding the reader that "...the philosophical schools of antiquity are thought-pictures reduced to their simplest forms: they are geometrical projections of the logical..." (p. 97). Given such, he posits the following: since mathematical constructs are a representation on some level of basic philosophical ideals, and building must adhere to mathematical laws, it is fitting to further understand Masonic tradition by delving into the history and symbolism of sacred numbers over the ages. Thus, this is the focus of his third Masonic lecture.

In Silberer's lecture entitled "III. Sacred Numbers" (*Psyche and Eros*, Vol. II, No. 2, Mar.–Apr. 1921), he posits three fundamental assumptions. First, that number symbolism has had a "psychic deeprootedness" (p. 82) that has passed down throughout the ages, and exists implicitly, covertly, and even overtly, today. Second, as he had noted elsewhere, symbols frequently represent the psyche's best effort at that moment of mankind's development to illustrate a construct which it is unable to fully grasp and articulate; and third, the symbolism of numbers has played a crucial role in this process.

He also once again displays his admiration for Freemasonry for its capacity to absorb key Hebraic, Christian, and even Gnostic principles, as well as "...elements of value in ancient Chaldean astrologic phantasy, in Hebraic cabalistic art, (and) in Pythagorean number-lore..." (p. 81). He notes that from the very beginning of such civilizations, "...sacred didactic images are constituted primarily of numbers, not forms..." (p. 82). Silberer then systematically outlines critical numbers over time, and their symbolic significance (e.g. *"one (1)* is unity, the undivided, pure Being, etc, and symbolized by the circle, the line etc.; *two (2)* is duality, division of the sensual vs. the spiritual, etc. and symbolized by two points, two lines, etc; *three (3)* is a level of insight and integration above duality, and symbolized by the trinity, the nuclear family, etc.). He further notes that in an effort to safeguard the depth of this special knowledge, and resist external threats to it, numeric symbols were gradually replaced by pictorial representations, especially of builder's tools (e.g. mason's square; hammer; compass with protractor; pickaxe; etc.), hence the extraordinarily rich, 'multiple determinants' of the Masonic lodge and the practice of Freemasonry.

Silberer's idealism and spiritual leanings are evidenced when he concludes the lecture by reminding the reader that such symbolism is in service of the Royal Art, the stuff of alchemy, or "...the so-called 'hermetic art'..." (p. 89). He poetically continues that the "...royal essence of this art [is] this art of self-determination, of leading the seekers to the sublime, of scattering the treasures of wisdom, of transforming slaves into freemen..." (p. 89) – and reaffirms his perspective that Freemasonry is a teeming crucible instrumental in fostering this art.

Silberer's final lecture, "The Symbols of Freemasonry" (*Psyche and Eros*, Vol. II, No. 5, Sept.–Oct. 1921) is comprehensive, wide-ranging, and provocative. He continues to exhaustively examine the nature of symbols, and even alludes to Freud's notion of libido. To begin, he reminds the reader that he is moving from his exploration of the meaning of the symbolism of numbers to look more closely at other fundamental symbols, particularly of death and light. In his introduction, Silberer lays the foundation for what he perceives as the relationship between these two critical symbols. Again, his spiritual disposition is apparent. He notes that in the earliest religious accounts, death was perceived as not only a dreaded, final place, but also a space of mysterious potential that promised growth through transformation. In his words, the "...upward striving man..." who is willing to engage in the "...psychologically necessary ... practices ... of purification or transformation..." is able to "...acquire great dignity..." (p. 299). He continues that "...we always find the idea that mankind which strives for a complete life must pass through death. The neophyte is transformed by means of a ritual which symbolizes dying; he discards his present life and is fitted for a *more perfect life*..." (p. 299, emphasis in original text). In discussing how widespread such a human drama has been over the ages, Silberer insightfully observes: "...The regularity of these typical forms, their ubiquity, the obstinacy with which they persist in the course of evolution, are facts which per se prove that there is a human necessity for them even if we cannot determine their psychological determinants..." (p. 300).

Again, linking his discussion to the world of Freemasonry, he adds "...I need hardly tell you that in the Masonic rituals we find all the aforementioned factors: departure, examination, death, light, gaining a new life (by 'rebirth' or inner transformation); that, in other words, the everlasting breath of the individual yearning for the higher life..." (p. 300). Silberer then proceeds to outline this central theme of transformation over the centuries.

In so doing, Silberer directly addresses the Freudian notion of libido. He asks:

> What is the deepest thing, the root-matter, the mysterious driving power, in all life? Surely, not virtue, not morality, not wisdom! It is a titanic savage will, the will to live, the will for pleasure! An uncontrollable primitive fire, dangerous, frightful, majestic, sensuous and wonderfully creative!
>
> (p. 302)

He recognizes this fire by the name given by Freud (libido) but takes issue with its fixed, only pleasure-seeking definition when he states: "... From this all-powerful primitive fire, burning in the soul of every living thing, the new life is derived by the wise art, the *royal art*..." (p. 302, emphasis added). Thus, Silberer proposes that masonry with its alchemical and hermetic roots, and its myriad of extraordinarily rich symbols and rituals, has the capacity to elevate the libidinally bound individual to a higher (royal? spiritual?) level of being. He affirms: "...this is quite clear: it is the task of the lodge (represented by its leader) to promote the process of illumination..." (p. 303).

As to symbolism's foundational role in the evolution of mankind, Silberer reflects:

> ...Symbols are unlimitable signs and yet must be apperceived they are inexhaustible, and yet we try to get all out of them. We may say, then, that they contain the everlasting should, the everlasting *prototype* ... By virtue of the *universal* language they speak, symbols are an integral part of the *kingly* art...
>
> (p. 304, emphasis added)

Silberer closes his lecture with an inspirational exhortation 'considering the inestimable value of symbols':

> ...may they who have been sacred to us for centuries, they to whom we owe so much, they who incorporate within themselves the wisdom of countless earnest spirits, continue to be sacred to us and illuminate like stars our paths which are not always easy and luminous but often quite difficult and dark...

(p. 304)

At the end of the above lecture published in *Psyche and Eros*, Silberer posted an addendum containing further reflections on symbolism, as well as some strikingly cogent comments related to Freudian and Jungian theory at the time. He begins by continuing his discussion of the necessity of rebirth as a requisite for self-betterment or self-renewal. Utilizing references ranging from John's Gospel (i.e. the story of Nicodemus) to rituals of passage employed by tribes in British East Africa (at the time), he underscores the related themes of death of the self; return to the mother; and then, rebirth as a vehicle of self-development, and individuation. He further explains: "...rebirth is one of the prerequisites for the mystic creation of the new man, and that one of the pre-requisites for this rebirth is introversion (which takes on the symbolic shape of finding a mother)..." (p. 306).

Silberer credits 'Dr. C. G. Jung of Zurich' for introducing the term 'introversion' defined as "...being lost in one's soul: withdrawing one's interest from the outer world and seeking out the treasures of one's own inner world..." (p. 306). He notes that both Jung and Freud present varied theories of the pathological introversion and resulting ailments including neurosis, or worse, dementia praecox. In a word, "... Introversion often presents itself as an abandonment of the (perhaps unattainable or troubled) pleasures of the outer world and a seeking out of libido sources within oneself..." (p. 306). Again, however, Silberer underscores the non-pathological trajectory of such introversion when speaking of spirituality:

> But castigation, or, at least abstemiousness, as well as the withdrawal from the outer world and turning to the inner world, are required by all the teachings leading to an intensive acceptance of religion, i.e. to mysticism, to the mystic life ... Religious experience in the form of introversion is mysticism...

(p. 306)

Silberer notes that churches and cloisters over the centuries "...with their mysterious darkness, their numerous columns, their richly pictorial symbols, [and] their music..." were [are] 'introversion institutions' teeming with imagery of dying and descending into the subterranean unknown (p. 306). Silberer labels such activity 'threshold symbolism', and connects this on an individual level with falling asleep and then awakening.

He adds that "...Introversion is always linked with *regression* ... a reversion to a more primitive mode of psychic activity, from thinking to picturing, from acting to hallucinating; a backward longing for childhood..." (p. 307, emphasis in original text). He notes that in this primitive mode of psychic activity, the preference is for symbolic modes of speech as well as infantile images, especially the mother-imago. He notes that psychoanalysis is the domain of exploration of childhood issues and conflicts. *Silberer then directly aligns with Jung opposed to Freud regarding the latter's cornerstone Oedipus complex.* He asserts:

> ...one must be careful not to interpret this Oedipus complex and the incest *too literally*; it must be borne in mind, as has been insisted on by Jung, that the incest is also only a figure, an image for a striving which leads the individual adapted to an active life back, as it were, into the convenient security found in one's mother, or in her lap...
>
> (p. 307, emphasis added)

Silberer then discusses his theory of 'elementary types'. He proposes that:

> ...the unconscious of all human beings is so much alike it follows that they all carry about within them many primitive, scarcely alterable images or schemata which are common to all. And inasmuch as symbolism is fed by these elementary types it is necessarily, without any external reasons, related to the inmost part of mankind...
>
> (p. 307)

He then fascinatingly relates the results of some of his 'lecanomancy' experiments: i.e. have a subject gaze into a basin filled with water and relate freely what they perceive. Silberer then illustrates some of his aforementioned universal symbols in their responses.

Thus, to conclude, Silberer's series of lectures on Freemasony enabled him to expand his earlier discussions of symbolism, and to link such directly to the symbol-rich environment of the Masonic lodge and its extensive history and traditions. It is erudite, informative, and compelling. It also reaffirms his notion of symbols as necessary expressions of ideas for which the individual, or the society, lacks the capacity to grasp at that moment in time. In addition, he exhibits his alignment with Jung on the notion of universal categories of experience (archetypes?) as well as the severe limitations of the Oedipal Complex as a cornerstone of human development – as espoused in Freudian theory.

These lectures also radiantly align with his panoramic theory of dream formation and their interpretation, which I will discuss in the next chapter.

7   The dream

According to Jacob Blauner (1955), Silberer's aforementioned book on dreams (*Der Traum*) "...was originally a lecture which Herbert Silberer gave in 1918 in Vienna and then enlarged and published that same year..." (p. 361). Blauner notes positively that in this work, Silberer "... gives here his important expansion and modification of Freud's views, *anticipating by decades a development of dream theory which has only lately come into its own...*" (p. 361, emphasis added). Curiously, however, although Blauner is clearly laudatory of the contributions of the "...bright insights of this brilliant mind..." (p. 361), it was somehow deemed acceptable to *selectively* translate the work, and omit numerous case examples, as well as Silberer's summary of Freudian theory.

The fact that the work languished in German (out of the mainstream of psychoanalysis proper) for close to four decades, and was only introduced in this somewhat piecemeal fashion, seems to further reflect the ostracism visited upon Silberer in his final years.

In spite of all of the above, the actual complete book is delightful, insightful, and very engaging. The present author had it translated in *its entirety* into English (Galsi 2017), which allows the reader the full experience of Silberer's theses, as well as the local flavor of his times reflected in his experiments, or dream examples. Accordingly, an overview of the book is in order.

Silberer introduces his work by noting that "The human mind has always found fascination in the mysterious, the puzzling – particularly the mysteries of the soul" (p. 2). He adds that there are those who "... relish the mysterious for its own sake..." and employ an "emotional approach"; while others seek to "...dissolve what is mysterious..." via a "...scientific understanding of the subject..." (p. 2). Silberer inserts the study of dreams into this realm of mystery. He then provides an overview of the mysterious nature of the dream over the centuries from those who "...have gone so far as to regard dreams as somehow superior to waking, to believe that dreams transport us to ethereal realms, and closer to some sort of world spirit..." (p. 3) to those who "...value dreams for their prophetic content..." (p. 5) to "...Today's occultists [who] hold a variety of beliefs about the interpretability of dreams as messages of a higher kind, which communicate about spatially and temporally remote realities..." (pp. 5–6).

In contrast, he observes that the scientific appraisal of dreams was initiated by Scherner, whose "...attempt at a grand system of dream symbolism is undoubtedly a little fantastic..." yet focused on the basic scientific premise that dream imagery was reflective of the particular body organ being stimulated (p. 6). Silberer adds that "...Scherner's theory was refined by the esthetician Johannes Wolkelt..." who unfortunately "...attracted little attention..." (p. 6). Silberer notes that "...the scientific 'interpretation' of dreams lay dormant until brought back to life once again by the Viennese psychopathologist Freud, this time for good..."; and that Freud "...gave a number of bold ideas of Nietzsche a scientific basis, and raised dream psychology to a level even he could not have predicted..." (pp. 6–7).

Silberer gives credit to Freud in the development of his own (Silberer's) ideas on dreams, but also makes it clear that he (Silberer) has also relied on his own research and experimentation to inform his theory. As to theory, he clarifies that he "...attempt(s) to avoid exaggerations that one tends to associate with some all-too-enthusiastic followers of the Freudian school (in a word, the 'psychoanalysts')... (p. 7).

To introduce his discussion of dreams, Silberer returns to the discovery that essentially elevated his profile in the psychoanalytic community back in 1909: the exploration of what he termed the 'hypnagogic phenonemon'. As the details of this (i.e. the material, functional, and somatic categories) have been discussed earlier in the current book, we will not delve into them at this time. However, at the end of his discussion, Silberer does add an observation that slightly expands his earlier exploration. Specifically, he notes that certain hypnagogic images "...belong in the realm of dreams..." (p. 15), and observes: "...Images that are symbolic of wakening are often to be found at the end of dreams..." (p. 15). One of the examples he employs to illustrate this is as follows: "...*Example 18 – End of Dream*: I arrive at my home accompanied by other people. I say goodbye to them outside the door, and enter – *Interpretation*: The return home signifies the approaching wakefulness" (p. 15).

Silberer also notes that certain researchers have posited that there is a "...relationship between hallucinations in half sleep and dreams..." (p. 16). In fact, Silberer opens a new window when he asserts that "...

hallucinations experienced in half sleep (which we can regard as *rudimentary dreams*) work to transform a thought, a feeling, condition, an impression into an image, or more precisely, a vivid episode..." (p. 16, emphasis added). He reminds the reader that:

...the process of visualization is also one of facilitating a form of thought which best manifests itself as the process of transforming a relatively taxing abstract thought process into simpler images. It is tiredness that forces the application of a more primitive form of thought...

(p. 17)

He also quotes some of Nietzsche's profound observations on the issue: "In sleep and in dreams we undertake anew early mankind's journey ... Dreams carry us back to the earlier stages of human culture..." (p. 17). Thus, exhaustion (negative factor) transforms a thought (positive factor) into the primitive imagery of the hypnagogic, and by extension, the dream. Silberer also underscores that 'affect' needs to be attached to the positive factor. He concludes: "...This emotional element is indispensable..." (p. 17).

Silberer continues to discuss the autosymbolic phenomenon in his next chapter. He cites Dr. Karl Schrotter's *experimental dreams*: dreams in which subjects were given suggestions in a deepened hypnotic state, and their imagery appeared to mirror such suggestions. Silberer also continues to survey the pervasiveness of somatic-induced imagery in dreams, including the fascinating self-experimentation of Trumbull Ladd in the optical realm. Silberer notes that Ladd:

...After some practice [was] able to wake himself without opening his eyes, 2–5 minutes after going to sleep; [and] had the opportunity to compare retinal impressions as they were vanishing to the dream images still in his memory [and] claims that in every case it was possible to establish an internal relationship between the two...

(p. 24)

Silberer concludes the chapter by noting that the "'painter' that creates hypnagogic hallucinations or dream images reaches for the colors that are most accessible to it. It appears to practice a certain economy in this. Dreams take the line of least resistance" (p. 25).

Silberer goes on in his next chapter to insightfully and commonsensically describe what he calls the instigator of dreams. For some reason, many of his examples did not make it into the aforementioned 1956 translation. He reminds the reader that the "…autosymbolic phemomenon, which, so far, we have assumed to be associated with dreams, may be taken to be products of a positive factor which is inhibited by a negative factor, and whose motive may be an affect, or an emotion, which, in a manner of speaking, demands attention…" (p. 26). He goes on to give an example of what he terms a *dream of intention*: i.e. the dream drama accomplishes a task that in reality would be difficult to do so. Included in such are what he defines as *dreams of convenience*, and explains that they "…include those well-known dreams that we sometimes have in the morning as we are trying to prolong sleep, and that represent us having already got up and dressed, and even having gone off to work…" (p. 27). Again, he offers intriguing examples of such that illustrate the psyche's capacity to spontaneously convert images in a manner that achieves this goal, as in the following example:

> …I am woken in the morning to the nearby tower clock striking 8. I realize with regret that I must get up soon. *Contemplation in half-sleep:* A way out occurs to me: why not represent 8 in the soprano clef instead of the treble clef: that way, it would be a 6, and I would have gained two hours…
>
> (p. 28)

Also included in such are the elaborate images produced to remind and/or partially satisfy physical needs for thirst or urination, etc. Silberer adds that in general, dreams of convenience might equally be called dreams of inconvenience since "…Obviously, our tendency, our *wish* in all of these dreams is to be rid of the inconvenience…" (p. 29).

Silberer then shifts into Freud's notion of the "…extraordinarily fruitful wish fulfillment theory of dreams…" (p. 30). He notes that historically over the centuries writers have hypothesized that, as I. G. E. Maab asserts:

> Experience confirms our view that we dream most frequently of the things on which our warmest passions are centered … The ambitious man dreams of the laurels he has won (or imagines he has won) or of those he has still to win; while the lover is busied in his dreams with the object of his sweet hopes…
>
> (p. 30)

Although Silberer credits Freud with confirming and elaborating on this invaluable notion, he takes issue when he observes that: "…Despite the neat example, there is an immediately obvious objection to the wish fulfillment theory of dreams: equally often we have dreams that are not to do with wish fulfillment, but rather exactly the opposite!" (p. 31).

Again, Silberer does acknowledge the insights of psychoanalysis as he articulates his positions. For example, he states: "…One might define psychoanalysis (which is also the ultimate means of investigating the dream) as a form of confessional with scientific grounding, where the mental and emotional inventory of the person under analysis is followed with unending patience to its last bifurcation…" (p. 33). He continues:

…The path is treacherous, as it leads into the private life of the individual. The hidden 'safes' of the soul … the sore spots of the psyche … those impulses, memories, and thoughts, that … run contrary to the person's morally upright (and sometimes conventional or somewhat of a Philistine) conscious, and thus result in an inner conflict…
(p. 33)

He agrees that "…The conflict may, under circumstances, may attain such magnitude as to result in neurotic conditions e.g. hysterical symptoms, obsessive thoughts, agoraphobia or claustrophobia, etc. – conditions that psychoanalysis seeks to identify the root of and heal…" (p. 33).

Silberer then departs from the classic Freudian stance when he asserts: "…it should be noted that the instigators of dreams need not necessarily be sought in the deepest layers of the psyche that hide in the darkness of the unconscious; on the contrary, they may be found on *any* level…" (p. 34, emphasis added). He continues that although "…they seldom lie close enough to the surface to be immediately visible…" and that there is typically an "…emotionally powerful instigator…":

I am not certain that there is justification for maintaining Freud's categorical claim that dreams only serve to represent a situation in which a wish is fulfilled. It is an aspect that may be generally relevant: the question is whether this is the only relevant aspect, whether there may not be other cases in which it is some other factor coexisting with the wish that plays a more significant role in the complex dream mechanism…
(p. 34)

Silberer concludes this provocative chapter as follows:

…While in agreement with the theory of repressed wishes and their unrecognizable manifestations, I wish to adopt a more general formulation, according to which the instigator of dreams is always an *emotionally hochwertig* (i.e. high value, high quality) factor, which arouses our interest with excitement or lack thereof, and brings us into a state of joyful expectation, smug self reflection, anxious fear, worried observation, bitter complaining, or in a state of inner activity animated by some other affect. Usually, there are multiple factors involved in a dream...

(p. 43, emphasis in original text)

He further notes that "...one and the same dream may lend itself to an equally rich functional and material interpretation..." (p. 43). (As an aside, it is probable that so clear a departure from Freudian orthodoxy was probably at least a part of the reason this work was not translated into English for almost half a century.)

In the next section of this work, Silberer more extensively details what he calls "The mechanism of dream formation". He begins by reiterating what he mentioned earlier: namely the frequent 'instigator' of dreams is the 'high value, high quality complex' – i.e. the 'sore spot' in our psyche that may have lingered since childhood. He notes that they can include all of the following and more:

...long forgotten painful experiences; long repressed infantile desires we are no longer consciously aware of; perverted drives that we have quelled but not vanquished; suppressed hateful and vengeful impulses; a love painfully torn from the heart; missed opportunities; ever-present guilt over a misdeed; doubts never lifted; [etc.].

(p. 44)

To support his case, he then presents a wide range of dreams as examples of this process. In so doing, he is careful to give Freud extensive credit for his notion of dreams as essentially 'wish fulfillment' experiences, as well as some of the more technical mechanisms such as *condensation* and *displacement*. He also concurs with Freud that dream work must operate within the *considerations of representability*: i.e. enactment and pictorial images. However, Silberer is also quite clear in his personal conviction that a dream symbol is frequently 'multiply determined' – there is not just one interpretation of it. In fact, he discusses one dream in which "...the incident with the deer compresses at least *six* strong emotionally charged lines of thought..." (p. 50, emphasis added). Additionally, in his discussion, he draws parallels with his earlier work on hypnagogic phenomena and the auto-symbolic process, and notes that dreams are full of *functional* and *material* symbolism. Throughout this part of the discussion, Silberer's tendency to ambitiously see numerous levels of meaning in dreams is apparent. Silberer then shifts into a lighter discussion of "Typical Dreams and Symbols". His fundamental reasoning is quite sound:

> ...Despite all the differences in individual experience, knowledge, and endeavor, there are many emotions, conflicts, physical experiences that are more or less common to all human beings. Since these emotional (and somatic) moments often feature in dreams, it is not surprising that there exist typical dreams that are commonly known...
>
> (p. 61)

He again offers examples and 'typical' categories of interpretations of such. These include: *dreams of flying* (sexual, somatic); *dreams of climbing stairs* (sexual); *dreams of falling* (anxiety); *dreams of being followed* (repressed instinct); and *animals in dreams* (passion). Silberer also credits Freud with observing that *dreams of being naked* trace back to infantile exhibitionism, and "...painful *dreams about the death of a person dear to one*, to repressed hostility towards them... (p. 63, emphasis added).

In the midst of this discussion, Silberer clearly posits two (clearly controversial at the time) caveats: "...one must not be tempted to interpret everything as sexual, as certain superficial followers of psychoanalysis appear committed to do..."; and *even more globally* "...we must not fail to note that there exist symbols with their own *individual characteristics*, that the same symbols may have *different interpretations*, and that the same thing can be expressed *through different symbols*, which makes things easier for the dreamer, if not for the interpreter..." (p. 64, emphasis added). He goes on to open up the discussion even further when he asserts (again, quite controversially):

> ...The fact that the dream has a repertoire of relatively self-evident symbols for various things, in addition to more random allusions, may be due to reasons similar to why we have stereotypical dreams – due to similar mental conditions, which may include, besides conceptual associations, also linguistic, conventional, even *vague mythological ones*...
>
> (p. 66, emphasis added)

Silberer then shifts focus and proceeds to explore the 'sometimes held' notion that dreams are "...capable of achievements, accomplishments, or performance which exceed the capabilities of the waking consciousness..." (p. 68). He posits one such instance as indisputable: "...dreams may sometimes produce *memories* which elude the waking consciousness..." (p. 68, emphasis in original text). He also notes that dreams are integrally entwined with the 'unconscious mind', and as such may "...reanimate infantile and other such 'fossilized' emotional content..." (pp. 67–68).

As to creative insights in dreams, Silberer is less optimistic. Similarly, with humor: "...jokes in dreams tend not to be particularly amusing. Gags that appear to be gags during a dream, and perhaps even upon waking, tend to reveal themselves as little more than indifferent puns or even tedious wordplay..." (p. 69). Although he acknowledges (with examples of dreams) the rare case when an individual has an extraordinary insight, or makes a profound insight in a dream, he asserts in general that: "...What appear to us brilliant thoughts and ideas tend to turn out to be trivial by the light of day – much as fairytale gold that turns to dust once you cart it home..." (p. 69).

Silberer then digresses briefly to explore the notion of somnambulism and its similarity to dreams. He summarizes this as follows: "...the sleepwalker, like a dreamer, is driven by a motive force whose main component is of an affective nature (wish, intention), and if the activity actually performed is accompanied by a subjective experience, i.e. a dream, then this motive force governs both..." (p. 73).

He also explores "...two wonderful properties, associated with dreams since ancient times, that today's occultists – to say nothing of the mindlessly superstitious – attribute to dreams: *prophesy and spatial clairvoyance...*" (p. 76, emphasis in original text). Silberer makes quick work of both, finding the former "somewhat questionable" and the latter "...so fantastic ..." (p. 76) that neither deserve serious attention. He does, however, equivocate on a third, related category, that of *telepathic dreams*, which he defines as "...The claim that a dreamer (and in certain circumstances also persons in a waking state) could be accessible to mental influence exerted by means other than sense perception..." using the analogy of the "...wireless telegraph..." (p. 77). He further explains: "...the phenomena that are under consideration here – communication about the dying, the sick, those in danger, the recognition of an attack, greeting someone who's returned without one's prior knowledge..." (p. 77). From a scientific vantage point, Silberer notes that there is no indisputable empirical data to confirm such claims. However, he asserts that he is familiar with such cases that are "...quite astonishing..." (p. 77), and acknowledges that "...there exist relevant experiences in such numbers as to convince the parties involved more than sufficiently..." (p. 77). However, he concludes that he has "...come to a veritable grave of personal conviction..." (p. 77) on the issue.

Along a similar vein, he then discusses the fact that the dream state is one of heightened sensitivity, and as such, "...tend to usher into the consciousness, [those] perceptions, stimuli, and impressions that escape the attention in the tumult of the day and hence remain unknown..." (p. 77). Silberer sees three general types of this process. First, he describes the awareness of the dreamer's *impending physical illness* as one such perception illuminated via the dream state. Additionally, subtle interpersonal interaction and *resulting impressions of other(s)* that may not have been registered in the conscious mind – may be illuminated in the dream state, and actually help guide the dreamer in his further conscious interactions with said individual(s). The third category is in service of self-reflection: "...this prophetic power lies in an ability to shine a light on the dreamer's own person ... reveal to him tendencies which might otherwise escape his attention; show him the motive force behind these tendencies; and more or less clearly, their goal" (p. 79).

Silberer concludes this work by discussing the notion that the dreamer is wholly 'responsible' for his dream. He quotes Nietzsche ("... Nothing contains more of your own work than your dreams..." p. 79); Tolstoy ("...My dreams, on the other hand, give me the yardstick that measures the stage of moral perfection that I have attained..." p. 80); and others on the subject. While somewhat sympathetic to the notion, he takes issue with the conclusion that the dream is absolutely the 'mirror of character'. He offers three qualifications. First, when somatic situations are so significantly problematic that they 'instigate' a dream with malignant figures, they cannot "...be ascribed to the dreamer's character..." (p. 81). Second, and similar, "...fears and unpleasant experiences from daytime existence..." (p. 81) that likewise create pernicious figures cannot be attributable to the dreamer's character. Third and probably most notably due to Silberer's understanding of, though obviously not blind adherence to, Freudian theory, "...often, a dream is not a confessor so much as it is a deceiver..." (p. 81) – making the mirror less than clear. He explains further: "...the dream may be the mirror of the soul, but not the dream that we see fleetingly, but the dream that we analyze..." (p. 82). He continues that such analysis involves both "...shining a light into the dark in the spirit of *truth*..."; and "...penetrat[ing] to terrifying depths into our Epicurean nature..." (p. 82).

Silberer's idealism grounded in stark realism is evident in the final page of this work. On the one hand, he notes that in dreams "...we make acquaintance with the shadows..." (p. 83). On the other hand, he poetically reminds us: "...Let us not forget the light side. Shadow and light complete each other in forming a complete picture of the character..." (p. 83). He continues that:

> ...it is a person's *actions* that must determine the moral judgement of his character. The base tendencies that the 'tricksy' dream images are wont to serve and yet are deeply repressed, away from the realm of deeds, are in a manner of speaking the fertilizer from which culture may blossom; they are the foundation on which we – with great effort – have built our character...
>
> (p. 83)

Therefore "...as regards dreams and the human character, we like to associate dreams with a valuable function: it is the *secret chamber of the psyche*..." (p. 83, emphasis added).

One element that Silberer curiously did not explicitly address in this little book on dreams was his somewhat signature issue of the anagogic level of dreams – an issue he proposed in *Problems of Mysticism and Its Symbolism.* A clear sticking point in the psychoanalytic craw, it was actually something Freud would directly and indisputably condemn – to ensure that his flock would not be misled. Perhaps this is why Silberer excluded it from so engaging and pleasant a book.

Silberer's reasoning on the anagogic is frankly an understandable extension of his appreciation of symbols and their frequent multiply determined status, with a somewhat mystical, transcendent overlay. His interest in the phenomenon centers on mankind's aspirations to create a pure substance (i.e. alchemy), and by extension find a 'higher' level of existence (i.e. Masonry). From this multiply determined, deeper, 'anagogic' level, symbols themselves reflected meaning, both personal and universal. Silberer proposes:

> ...the anagogic interpretation, whose alignment with the psychoanalytic seemed so impracticable, is a form of functional interpretation, or at least related to it. In this case it would at once be comprehensible how a product of the imagination harmonizes with several expositions (problem of multiple interpretation); because this variety of sense had already operated in the selection of the symbol and indeed, in those cases as well where we did not at first sight suspect the cooperation of the anagogic thoughts; secondly, the anagogic and the psychoanalytic interpretations are somehow reconciled to each other, whereby possibly also the position of the natural science interpretation can be made somewhat clearer...
>
> (pp. 112–113)

He continues by noting that while the psychoanalytic interpretation focuses on conflicts of the past, "...the anagogic image appears on the contrary to point to a state or process that is to be experienced in the future..." (p. 113).

Stretching things even further, Silberer adds "...in the case of every symbolism tending to *ethical development*, the anagogic point of view must be considered..." (pp. 118–119, emphasis added) – possibly linking this expanded level of interpreting dream symbols with an advance in the moral development of the species. Thus, when considering the psychoanalytic and the anagogic viewpoints, he summarily asserts that "...the treatment of symbolism from the two points of view must be superior to the one-sided treatment..." (p. 118).

Clearly, Silberer's panoramic understanding of dreams and their possible meanings was groundbreaking, almost breathtaking – especially for his time. Perhaps, it partially reflected his unique vantage point in the balloon, a place where 'altitude' and human potential might have synergistically fused in his psyche.

It also sadly suggests how desperate the earthbound, psychoanalytic community must have been to snuff out such optimistic heresy. In fact, one might argue that it took *psychoanalysis proper* almost three quarters of a century to begrudgingly acknowledge some of what Silberer proposed. For example, Kohut's (1977) notion of the 'self state' dream; Fosshage's (2002) 'revised model' of the psychological functioning of dreaming; and Weiss and Sampson's (1986) exposition of the 'higher mental functions' of dreaming, all illustrate how psychoanalysis has come around to a less drive-directed, more expansive notion of dream symbols, and their interpretation.

Needless to say, Jungian thought (Kalsched 2013; Whitmont & Perera 1989; Mattoon 1984; etc.), and frankly mainstream psychology, as well as 'main street' popular culture, have been there for quite a long time.

8   Silberer and psychoanalysis

Given the fact that the backdrop of Silberer's wide-ranging theories was the nascent field of psychoanalysis in the early decades of the twentieth century, his personal and theoretical connection to the theory, and its theorists, was extensive. As noted elsewhere, he very much wanted to be a psychoanalyst, but almost naively seemed to believe that he could be such, and reconcile the ideals of Freemasonry, as well as the insights of alchemy, in the process. Although it appears he proceeded in earnest and with much enthusiasm, at every turn, he was castigated, thwarted, or rebuked.

Yet amazingly, and again, perhaps because he had seen life and the world from a literally 'higher' vantage point, he remarkably plodded on. From his initial, almost apologetic attempt to do homage to the psychoanalytic tradition as he dissected the parable in *Problems of Mysticism and Its Symbolism*, to his more mature thinking on a wide range of topics in his work in *Psyche and Eros*, psychoanalysis was always a reference point, or backdrop, to be considered in the discussion. Unfortunately, it appears that his ultimate failure to remain in the good graces of this psychoanalytic movement was the 'instigator' of his own untimely death. Thus, before ending our exploration of his work, a closer look at his attempt to psychoanalytically understand the aforementioned Rosicrucian parable, as well as a sampling of some of his more mature works in *Psyche and Eros* is in order. We begin with the parable.

Silberer states that this parable needs to be viewed in the threefold manner that dreams are typically understood. First, from their "...typical dream images ... built on universal human emotions..." (p. 27). Second, "...from folk psychology ... the productions of the popular imagination and vice versa..." (p. 27). Third, by studying "...the peculiarities of the structure of the dream [where] one generally finds motives that are several times repeated in similar stories..." (p. 27).

Thus, by looking at the parable via these "...three methods of interpretation conjointly..." (p. 28), Silberer believes that he "...shall proceed *exactly as psychoanalysis does* in interpretation of folklore..." (p. 28), although he is careful to insert the qualifying "...I must treat some of the conclusions of psychoanalysis *with reserve* as problematic..." (p. 28, emphasis added).

Silberer then attempts to draw certain parallels between symbols and actions contained in the parable and psychoanalytic themes and constructs. For example, entering into the forest symbolically reflects delving into a deeper transitional state, not unlike his description of the hypnagogic, and even the image of the forest itself carries the aura of the hidden (unconscious?), or the mysterious. As to the fact that the wanderer in the dream meets a group of wise old men who insist that he (the wanderer) needs to undergo and survive a challenging 'ordeal' in order to be accepted by them, Silberer notes: "...obstacles in the dream correspond to conflicts of will on the part of the dreamer..." (p. 29). He continues: "...Anxiety develops when a suppressed impulse wishes to gratify itself, to which impulse another will, something determined by our culture, is opposed prohibitively", and asserts "...Only when the impulse in question knows how to break through without the painful conflict, can it attain pleasure..." (p. 29). Thus, from a Freudian perspective, the parable (as in all dreams) illustrates a "...tendency from anxiety towards the untroubled fulfillment of wishes..." (p. 29).

Silberer continues by noting that the parable is reminiscent of the 'graduation' dreams written about by Freud as well as Stekel, in which the central underlying drama revolves around the sexual potency of the dreamer. Relatedly, the challenge of scaling the steep wall also "...is used principally with reference to sexual excitements [in which] the right signifies a permitted (i.e., experienced by the dreamer as permissible), the left, an illicit sexual pleasure..." (p. 31). The wanderer's victory over the lion, and his eventual entry into the beautiful rose garden in which he encounters a "...most beautiful maiden arrayed in white satin with the most stately youth who was in scarlet ... going out of this lovely garden into our chamber to enjoy the pleasures of love..." (p. 31) symbolizes the "...complete fulfillment of wishes, the longing for love and power has attained its end..." (p. 31).

Quite ambitiously, Silberer clarifies that although such analysis might lead one to believe that the "...psychoanalytic solution of the parable was ended...", in fact, "...we have interpreted only the upper stratum..." (p. 32). Within the standard latent/manifest content frame, he attempts to sort out what forbidden impulses/desires are guarded against by the dream censor in this parable. He rules out homosexuality and exhibitionism, and arrives at *incest*, as the repressed dream wish. He then proceeds to review the parable's narrative from this perspective. In so doing, he embarks on lengthy tangents, and characteristically recounts related themes in myths from around the globe. His analysis might be considered wild and somewhat unfocused, yet his effort to clearly adhere to, and further enunciate, the psychoanalytic understanding of dreams is apparent.

Salient in this lengthy discussion are all the following parallels: the narrow path overgrown with bushes is the female body; the underworld, the uterus of the mother; the paradise, incest; the ordeal, fear of impotence; the assembly of elders, the father to be conquered; the red and white roses, sexuality; the breaking of flowers, masturbation; revivification of the merged and disintegrated lovers via the waters of life; and finally, the re-creation of the dismembered son who through union with the mother emerges as a more capable, 'kingly' victor – greater than the father (i.e. an Oedipal success). As noted elsewhere, Silberer asserts that the dream (parable) "...carries the wish fulfillment to the uttermost limits..." (p. 52). As noted, in his wide-ranging discussion of such themes, he also cites myths from Iran, China, Austria, etc, as well as the writings of Freud, Jung, Stekel, and Rank.

At the admitted risk of possibly being too general, he sums up his psychoanalytic understanding of this parable as follows:

> ...the wanderer in his phantasy removes and improves the father, wins the mother, procreates himself with her, enjoys her love even in the womb and satisfies besides his infantile curiosity while observing procreative process from the outside. He becomes King and attains power and magnificence, even superhuman abilities...
>
> (p. 55)

If Silberer achieved his goal of accurately depicting the psychoanalytic position in a manner that actually *pleased* his Freudian peers remains to be seen.

However, what is clear is that once done with it, he shifted into the more esoteric pursuits that he clearly viewed as an adjunct of, or more probably, an enrichment of, the psychoanalytic position. For example, he enters into the related discussions of alchemy and Masonic writings – both reviewed earlier in this book. He then embarks on an exploration of more mystical topics (e.g. *Introversion and Regeneration*; *The Royal Art*; and *The Goal of the Work*), and in so doing, departs from the psychoanalytic framework – especially in his enthusiastic endorsement of the aforementioned concept of the 'anagogic'. He applies it not only to dream interpretation but also the understanding of myth and fairy tales.

In fact, when he addresses what he calls *"The Problem of Multiple Interpretation"* in understanding the parable specifically, and analogous phenomena (e.g. dreams) in general, he asserts:

> ...The interpretations are really three: the psychoanalytic, which leads us to the depths of the impulsive life; then the vividly contrasting hermetic religious one, which as it were, leads us up to high ideals and which I shall call shortly the *anagogic*; and the third, the chemical (natural philosophical), which so to speak, lies midway ... between the psychoanalytic and the anagogic, and can, as alchemistic literature shows, be conceived as the bearer of the anagogic...
>
> (p. 102, emphasis added)

To bolster his position, Silberer references his detailed work on the hypnagogic phenomena, and the nature of the symbols formed: particularly the *functional* (the manner in which consciousness functions) and the *material* (the content of such consciousness and, at times, of the unconscious). He goes on to note the multiple interpretations implicit in the psychoanalytic concept of *condensation*, as well as the fact that "...symbols which were originally material pass over to functional use ... on the path of a determination inward or intro-determination..." (p. 112). He further explains that "...the anagogic interpretation ... is a form of functional interpretation, or at least related to it..." (p. 112). In fact, "...the anagogic has some part in the creation of the functional ... and ... appears ... to point to a state or process that is to be experienced in the *future*..." (p. 113, emphasis added); or in other words:

> ...We have to regard not merely whence we come but also whither we go ... ontogenetically as well as phylogenetically ... those symbols or frequently disguised images ... that besides representing 'titanic' tendencies ... are fitted to represent the anagogic...
>
> (p. 117)

Silberer continues: "...phantasy creations carry two meanings, the psychoanalytic and the anagogic ... the two meanings correspond to two aspects or two evolutionary phases of a psychic inventory of powers, which are attached as a unity to symbolic types..." (p. 148). He idealistically adds when discussing the interpretation of fairy tales: "... The anagogic interpretation is indeed a prospective explanation in the sense of an ethical advance. Now the evolution even of fairy tales shows quite clearly a progression towards the ethical..." (p. 150).

Silberer observes: "...natural philosophy appears to be the carrier, or the stalk on which the titanic and the anagogic symbolism blossoms. Thus, it becomes intelligible how the alchemistic hieroglyphic aiming chiefly at chemistry, adapted itself through and through to the hermetic anagogic educational goal..." (p. 149); and asserts: "...The necessity of reckoning with an anagogic content of myths results from the fact that religions with their ethical valuations, have developed from *mythical beginnings*..." (p. 152, emphasis added).

Thus, this demonstrable adherence to this additional 'anagogic' level of analysis (of dreams, myths, and symbols in general) set Silberer apart from the psychoanalytic credo of the time. He went even further afield when he proposed that the true purpose of the work of self discovery/analysis (i.e. as in psychoanalysis) is: "...To be sure the final outcome of the work can be summed up in three words: Union with God..." (p. 153). He supports this position by numerous references including: Kant's sense of duty; E. A. Hitchcock's work on the spiritual; and a host of mystical, religious, and alchemical writings that underscore the centrality of patience, love, and truth in pursuit of divine union. In fact, Silberer almost mystically proposes that: "The desired completion or oneness should be a state of the soul, a condition of being, not of knowing..." (p. 155), and explains further that the "... goal of the work [is] the recovery of the harmonious state of the soul..." (p. 167). He also unapologetically observes: "...As for the metaphysical import of the mystical doctrine, I might maintain that the psychoanalytic unmasking of the impelling powers *cannot prejudice its value*..." (p. 168, emphasis added).

Thus, what begins as a conciliatory effort to appease psychoanalysis transforms into a full-blown treatise on his proposed spiritual amendment to its efforts. This is further illustrated in the final section of the work entitled "The Royal Art". It is mostly a recounting of the spiritual odyssey of the mystic, Jane Leade, as well as some of the writing of Swiss Masonic author, Oswald Wirth, and author Robert Fischer. Silberer begins his discourse by underscoring the centrality and universalism of symbolism, and noting that the pursuit of self-perfection needs to be intimately entwined in it. He asserts that "...Symbolism ... is the most universal language that can be conceived..." (p. 169). Referencing C. G. Jung, Silberer adds "...everyone will find something appropriate to himself in the symbols, and I emphasize[d] the great constancy of the types fast rooted in the unconscious, types which impart to them a universal validity..." (p. 169).

As to the 'Royal Art' itself, Silberer outlines the trajectory followed in this work. He notes that: "...In regard to the high ethical aspirations of alchemy, we understand that as a mystic art it preserves those attributes of a royal art ... that of the perfection of mankind..." (p. 171). He further clarifies that: "Today, too, there is a royal art. Freemasonry bears this name. Not only the name but its ethical ideal connects it with the spirit of the old alchemy...", and cites Fischer's description of Freemasonry "... as a society of men who have set themselves the severe task of a wise life and labor as the most difficult task, of self-knowledge, self-mastery and self-improvement..." (p. 171).

Referencing Wirth, Silberer notes "...the work is divided into three main steps, which begin with the purifying, turn towards the inner soul, and end with the death-resembling Unio Mystica ... the unattainable ideal, which like a star in heaven shall give a sure course to the voyage of our life..." (p. 185). Quoting Fischer again, Silberer writes:

> ...Freemasonry rests on symbols and ceremonies; in that lies its superior title to continued existence. They are created for eternal verities and peculiarly adapted thereto; they are fitted to every grade of culture, indeed to every time, and do not fall like other products of the time, a sacrifice to time itself...
>
> (p. 186)

Silberer concludes this work in characteristically idealistic fashion when he writes:

> To each person symbols represent his own truth. To every one they speak a different language. No one exhausts them. Every one seeks his ideal chiefly in the unknown. It matters not so much what ideal he seeks, but only that he does seek one. Effort itself, not the object of effort, forms the basis of development. *No seeker begins his journey with full knowledge of the goal...*
>
> (p. 186)

Thus, although Silberer attempted to satisfy competing camps in his major work, he could not help but stray into the spiritual and metaphysical, and possibly invalidated his psychoanalytic contribution in the process. It should be noted that after this early, major work, Silberer continued to comment on major issues in general, and psychoanalysis in particular – especially in the journal of which he was co-editor for almost three years: *Psyche and Eros*. An overview of a sampling of such writings will 'round out' our discussion of Silberer's portfolio.

For example, in the first volume of the first edition of *Psyche and Eros* (Vol. I, No. 1, July 1920, pp. 53–57), Silberer critically reviewed the German translation of Ernest Jones' *The Theory of Symbolism*. Silberer posits that although Jones "...aims at 'attaining a fuller understanding of the theoretical nature of symbolism' as well as at determining exactly what may be regarded as a symbol..." (p. 53), "...His efforts ... are manifestly influenced and guided by the conclusion he wishes to reach..." (p. 53) and his "...essay ... illuminates only a particular and limited aspect of symbolism..." (p. 53). Silberer goes on to point out that Jones misunderstands and/or simplifies the nature of symbolism, and appears to have one predetermined goal: "...[to] bring the whole subject of symbolism under the sovereignty of the repression theory..." (p. 54).

Or in other words, "...symbolism arises as the result of intrapsychical conflict between the repressing tendencies and the repressed..." (p. 55). Silberer clearly takes issue with Jones' very narrow definition of symbolism, as well as the examples Jones utilizes to support his thesis. To the contrary, Silberer asserts his broader, more optimistic, stance on the process of symbolism: "...namely, the creation of visible images for lofty, abstract ideas, e.g. symbols of infinity, perfection of the universe, omnipotence, unity, duality, sovereignty, causality, nature, the animal, the spiritual, the growth of the soul, periodicity, the passion of love..." (p. 56). Silberer believes that although what Jones says about the "... finer details of repression is more or less true..." (p. 57), Jones has "... erred in his one-sided emphasis, an error which has seriously distorted the whole subject of symbolism [and] has wholly missed the intellectual and the ethical aspects of symbolism which makes it of such great interest in the history of philosophy" (p. 57).

Quite strikingly, however, Silberer very briefly somewhat retracts (*Psyche and Eros*, Vol. II, No. 4. Jul.–Aug. 1921, p. 249) the above-noted criticism of Jones' narrow treatment of symbolism after reading Jones' original English-version book. Silberer states that although "...I do not think that Jones's treatment of the subject fell out happily..." (p. 249), he (Silberer) was pleased that the English version "...deals at considerable length with an aspect of symbolism, viz.: functional symbolism..." (p. 249) that was left out of the apparently abridged German version. Why such abridgment(censorship?) occurred remains a mystery.

Also in *Psyche and Eros* (Vol. I, No. 3, Nov.–Dec. 1920, pp. 137–139), in a brief article entitled "The Steinach in Mythology", Silberer insightfully discusses the sexual gland transplanting experiments of Viennese biologist, Professor Steinach, in the context of the mythological themes of rejuvenation. Silberer notes "...two types of mythological expression: (1) The preservation of the life of man through the eating of certain substances; and (2) the reconstruction of the body after dissolution or after being swallowed (by monsters)..." (p. 137). He notes that the first type is typically aligned with the story of Eden, and the eating of the fruit of 'the tree of life', the apple of knowledge (including the Biblical definition of 'knowing'), and the fact that the apple is also seen as a "...sex symbol, principally because of its universal poetical identification with the breasts of woman..." (p. 138). He further notes that throughout mythology, "...Man seeks to make himself resemble nature and to augment and increase his fertility in primitive rites symbolic of sex..." (p. 138). As to the second type of mythological pursuits of regeneration, and the failures of such, Silberer cites the Argonautic tale of Pelias, who was "...cut into small pieces and boiled by his daughter in behalf of his rejuvenation..." as well as that of 'aging' Paracelsus who '...bade his servant cut him into pieces, place these pieces in a chest, and bury the chest in horse dung [for] exactly nine months..." (p. 139).

Silberer's point in his brief review is one of sobriety and caution. He asserts: "...These mythological limitations of human possibilities should not hinder us from putting hope and energy into unsounded channels, but they should serve as a moral to keep us from *childishly overestimating the unattainable*..." (p. 139, emphasis added).

In a later writing, Silberer overviews the works of three authors (Emil Lorenz's "The Political Myth, Problem, and Preliminary Communications"; Dr. Paul Federn's "The Psychology of the Revolution: The Fatherless State"; and A. Kolnai's "Psycho-analysis and Sociology") in an article entitled "Sociology, Politics, and Psychoanalysis" (*Psyche and Eros*, Vol. III, No. 1, Jan.–Feb. 1922, pp. 55–61). In it, Silberer explores some key connections between fundamentals of psychoanalysis and politics. One area of focus involves a lengthy exploration of the classic, early emergence of the punitive paternal leader of early primitive tribes, his eventual loss of power, and then the harsh fate (including cannibalism) visited upon him on their demise. In another area of focus, and frankly a theme prescient of terrible things that would eventually occur in Germany, Silberer expands upon Dr. Lorenz's observation of the centrality of unconscious forces in politics. Silberer insightfully observes:

> ...political upheavals – and, ultimately all occurrences in the history of mankind – cannot be adequately explained by the manifest external conditions nor by the reasonable grounds for the political occurrences, no matter how loudly these are asserted or how acceptable they may seem to the understanding which loves uncomplicated matters. To a very large extent, on the contrary, irrational

emotional factors are the active driving forces, and occasionally
they are so dominant that they bring about that for which the
rational explanation is only, as it were, a framework and to a certain
extent the subsequent justification required by the critical mind...

(p. 57)

He continues:

...these immeasurable and non-calculable forces exert their influence in large part from the Unconscious of mankind ... the non-
rational factors ... bring about surprises; they impart a mysterious
compelling force to the great upheavals, urge eruptively to action,
or in some mysterious way serve to inhibit actions which from a
rational viewpoint would appear to be unmistakably necessary...

(p. 57)

Before concluding the piece, Silberer assesses Kolnai's observation
that social revolutions that result in socialist or communist societies
are actually *regressive*, producing "...a certain state of undifferentiated
rawness [that involves] the obliteration of the individual ... and tends
towards a structurally obliterative uniformity..." (p. 59).

In another review, Silberer exhibits a level of respect and restraint
when in *Psyche and Eros* (Vol. III, No. 2, Mar.–Apr. 1922, pp. 112–116)
he discusses Freud's journal article "Crowd Psychology and Ego-analysis"
(Internat. Psychi. Verlag, Vienna, 1921; 800, p. 140). He succinctly
reports on Freud's discussion of crowd psychology, which Freud openly
acknowledges is based on Le Bon's book entitled *The Psychology of
Crowds*. However, at the end of this brief review, Silberer notes that
although:

...I have hitherto restricted myself to giving the reader of this
review as faithful an account of the contents of Professor Freud's
fascinating theme. I could have pursued a more critical course ...
[for example] ... One might attempt a defence of the primary herd
instinct which Freud repudiates. One might object to his theory of
suggestion, and could criticize more sharply his 'libidinous' bonds...

(p. 115)

In 'diplomatic' mode, Silberer settles on only mildly and obliquely
questioning the first two of these issues, and does so almost apologetically.

However, Silberer is not as restrained in his article entitled "Beyond Psychoanalysis" (*Psyche and Eros*, Vol. II, No. 3, May–Jun. 1921, pp. 142–151) – a response to Freud's *Beyond the Pleasure Principle*. In fact, it reflects one of Silberer's most direct challenges to Freudian theory. To begin, Silberer questions what appears to be Freud's 'eleventh hour' amendment of his psychoanalytic theory. Specifically, the insertion of an underlying instinct for inertia (i.e. death) into what had been the pillars of psychoanalysis (i.e. the pleasure principle and the reality principle) appears illogical and empirically unfounded. Silberer notes:

> The proponent of this idea is no other than Freud ... He ventures upon an astonishing salto by setting up *impulses for death*; nay, more; he brands all the impulses of living organisms as impulses for death and makes only one exception – which ultimately turns out to be no exception...
>
> (p. 143, emphasis in original text)

Silberer is additionally troubled by Freud's notion that the core reason for the 'repetition compulsion' is likewise to return the organism to inert, non-being. To counter this amendment to Freudian theory, Silberer attempts to amass perspectives that support the positive teleological trajectory of existence, including the Darwinian notion of purposeful, natural selection; as well as the goal and end product of sexuality: the *creation* (not cessation) of life.

By offering a relevant albeit not robust analogy, Silberer likewise takes issue with Freud's position that even the instinct of self-preservation exists only to enable the organism to choose *how it will die*:

> ...We may compare this to a man who begins with nothing and gradually accumulates riches, not for the purpose of wasting them, but of saving them. Of such a one Freud would hardly wish to say that in the beginning *he was really striving to possess nothing*...
>
> (p. 147, emphasis added)

Silberer states further that: "...the effect of the instincts is undoubtedly improved adaptation to life; to attribute death, the end of life, to the instincts would be pure arbitrariness..." (p. 147). He additionally takes issue with Freud's dismissal of Woodruff's protozoa experiment – generally accepted as an illustration of the "...asserted immortality of living matter" (p. 148). Freud's notion that the experiment's results were merely a by-product of the positive, renewing, experimental conditions, and not a true test of the organisms' wish to cease existence, was seen by Silberer as incorrect. Silberer asserts:

> Thus we see that the protozoa do all that is in their power to remain alive! If a man were to be shut into a diving bell in which the air is not renewed he would die of suffocation; but would it follow that he had an instinct for death?
>
> (p. 149)

Silberer notes that Freud has regrettably "...lost himself in the impenetrable thicket [with] no earthly way out..." (p. 150) when he attempts to merge the sadistic element of sexuality with this newly proposed death instinct. He (Silberer) goes on somewhat in exasperation when he notes that: "...Not that I mean to imply that Freud is not himself a master; but it is on firm ground of empirical knowledge that he rules, sometimes *despotically*. His admirable powers lie within the bounds of psychoanalysis, not beyond it..." (pp. 150–151, emphasis added). He continues:

> ...The whole of Freud's thought-structure (after all only a house of cards?), the pinnacle of which ominously terminates in a death-instinct, is really built on the narrow foundation of a single pecu-liarity to be observed in the treatment of neurotics at the stage of transference...
>
> (p. 151)

Silberer eloquently concludes his review with his balanced position on the issue. He writes:

> The important role attributed to the surprising conception of death-instincts may finally lead us to ask whether such instincts really exist. They certainly do ... often enough manifested in life and in art. But these *impulses* cannot be called instincts, nor can they be considered something of a *primary* nature ... keep in mind [that] Consciousness [has] fulfilled its purpose as *no other* quality of living substance had done before ... *beyond* its biological purpose, became independently dominant and succeeded in setting itself up over the biological purpose ... [therefore] death impulses ... are late blossoms on an old stem – reversal phenomena *running counter* to the natural impulses. They are manifestations of consciousness which have become independent and *foreign* to the biological goals.
>
> (p. 151, emphasis added)

Thus, as noted above, Silberer's writings were wide-ranging, creative, and insightful. He initially aimed to defer to, or integrate his thinking with, psychoanalytic theory. However, as time progressed, he appeared to become more comfortable with directly challenging such.

As observed repeatedly, such 'oppositional' behavior was clearly not well received. From Jones' observation of Silberer's 'philosophic virus'; to Freud's 'despotic' refusal to continue contact with him; to the severe criticism he suffered at the hands of the Vienna Group (especially his last presentation), Silberer was consistently rejected by the psychoanalytic community.

A final illustration of how pointed and absolute such criticism could be is seen in Freud's *categorical* dismissal of Silberer's central notion of the anagogic, reflected in the following (from "Dreams and Telepathy", *Studies in Parapsychology*, 1963):

> ...As you know, Silberer, who was among the first to issue a warning to us on no account to lose sight of the nobler side of the human soul, has put forward the view that all or nearly all dreams permit such a twofold interpretation, a purer, *anagogic* one beside the ordinary psychoanalytic one. This is, however, *unfortunately not so*; on the contrary, a further interpretation of this kind is rarely possible; there has been *no valuable example* of such a dream-analysis with a double meaning published up to the present time within my knowledge.
>
> (p. 84, emphasis added)

Thus, it is unfortunately quite understandable that Silberer, who so treasured idealism and the transcendent, would become demoralized, and even despondent, after being subjected to such continuous, destructive criticism by the very group with whom he hoped to closely affiliate.

9 An appraisal of Silberer's contributions

One might inquire: given the fact that the field of psychoanalysis (fragile as it may be at present), and psychotherapy in general, have proceeded along essentially without explicitly acknowledging Silberer for close to a century, are his contributions so important that they should be reviewed?

It is the hope of this author that the present work has given the reader enough exposure to Silberer's thinking to answer the question in the affirmative – particularly given the fact he was writing over a century ago, when the giants of psychoanalysis were only beginning to fathom the awesome implications of the unconscious. The fact that his voice was cruelly silenced does not justify continued shunning.

Additionally, Silberer really was a brilliant theorist, and his observations clearly contributed to, if not ignited, some of the insights in psychoanalysis at the time, as well as psychology to this day. From such a vantage point, let me suggest at least eight reasons why Silberer's work deserves renewed attention:

- First, his careful study of his own thought processes in the tradition of the true scientists of the past resulted in his very compelling, very logical, and very widely accepted (even by Freud) description of *hypnagogic phenomena* replete with his functional, content, and somatic delineations. This, alone, merits more than a passing footnote.
- Second, his comprehensive assessment and understanding of the depth and complexity of *symbols*, and their relevance to mythology and dream imagery, was groundbreaking and impressive at the time, and still demands our attention.
- Third, his encyclopedic knowledge of the history and function of *alchemy*, and its relationship to psychological reality, was unique at the time, and is still fascinatingly informative. Again, recall Jung's acknowledgment of so grand a contribution.

- Fourth, and related to the previous two points, it should be noted that Silberer was clearly what would be called an Integrative Psychologist today. Not only did he mesh the literal heavens via balloon flight with the earthly world of drive theory, he also attempted to integrate the genesis and meaning of symbols with the rich tradition of *Freemasonry*. His lectures on Masonry and its symbols are rich, erudite, and instructive.

- Fifth, and *perhaps most compelling*, his theory of *dreams* and their interpretation is wide-ranging, refreshing, and extremely engaging. Although he initially went through much effort to adhere to the narrowly defined Freudian model, his illuminating personal experience; his knowledge of history, philosophy, and symbolism; and his appreciation of the awesome depth of the human psyche, clearly inspired him to 'open up the window', and allow air and light into the dreary Freudian metaphysic of the period. Not only did he elevate dream symbols to 'multiply determined' entities that were so much more than 'disguise work', he also advocated for a more timeless, possibly transcendent, 'anagogic' level that linked mankind together over the centuries, and possibly allowed for an 'ethical advance' of the particular individual, as well as the species in general. Jungian dream interpretation theory; Kohut's 'self state dream'; and Fosshage's 'revised model of dream interpretation' are just a few of the modern examples that mirror Silberer's position. Even Silberer's concept of the anagogic sounds very similar to notion of 'the leading edge' in Self Psychology: i.e. the notion that dreams not only reflect the 'situation as is' (in Jungian terms), but also offer guidance and direction as to what next steps the dreamer might take in his or her life. Thus, as Blauner (1955) noted, Silberer has played a *major* (though mostly unrecognized) *foundational role* in how dreams are understood and interpreted to this very day!

- Sixth, and possibly enhanced by his literal exposure at the time to the glories of being among the clouds on his balloon flights, Silberer's writings reflect a consistently *optimistic tone* that looked toward the future, and was not mired in past determinants. Such a hopeful teleological stance has parallels with the Human Potential Movement; Humanistic ('Third Force') Psychology; Positive Psychology; and even Mindfulness Theory.

- Seventh, Silberer clearly embraced the notion that human beings as a species were *evolving*, and not just on a physiological, 'survival of the fittest' level. Rather, he also envisioned the human species evolving in terms of *consciousness and awareness*, not unlike the theories of process philosopher Alfred North Whitehead, or process theologian, Teilhard de Chardin. Silberer's framing of mythology as being essentially the best a culture can do at a given point in time to understand a given idea, due to the culture's *limited cognitive capacity at the time* in history, is an elegant example of this 'evolution of consciousness' construct.

- Eight and last, Silberer's acceptance, and frankly at times, robust endorsement of, *transcendence and spirituality*, as well as his consistent effort to try to merge the worlds of psychology and spirituality, was extremely controversial at the time – and clearly contributed to his alienation (e.g. Freud's dismissal of Silberer: "The man is a Jesuit"). However, not surprisingly, there exists a movement in psychology and psychotherapy today to pursue this very same marriage of the psychological and the spiritual, when doing so enhances the healing process of a given individual.

Thus, in closing, it is definitely the position of this writer that Herbert Silberer *does* deserve his *day in court*.

In fact, when all is said and done, I believe he will be appreciated as one of the early psychoanalytic pioneers at the beginning of the twentieth century whose contributions remain instructive and of value today.

References

Angelergues, J. (2005) Anagogical interpretation. *International Dictionary of Psychoanalysis*. Retrieved May 15, 2015 from www.encyclopedia.com/topic/Anagogical_Interpretation.aspx.

Fosshage, J. L. (1989) The organizing function of dream mention. Retrieved July 6, 2015 from www.psychomedia.it/rapaport-klein/fosshage02.htm

Freud, S. (1963) Dreams and telepathy. In *Studies in Parapsychology*, New York: Collier Books.

Jung, C. G. (1955–1957) Mysterium Conjuntionis: An inquiry into the separation of psychic opposites in alchemy. *Collected Works*, Vol. 14, London: Routledge & Kegan Paul.

Kalsched, D. (2013) *Trauma and the Soul: A Psycho-Spiritual Approach to Human Development and its Interruption*, New York: Routledge.

Kohut, H. (1977) *The Restoration of the Self*, New York: International Universities Press, Inc.

Mattoon, M. A. (1986) *Understanding Dreams*, Dallas, TX: Spring Publications, Inc.

de Mijolla, A. (2005) Silberer, Herbert (1882–1923). *International Dictionary of Psychoanalysis*. Retrieved July 6, 2015 from www.encyclopedia.com/doc/1G2-3435301369.html

Nitzschke, B. (1997) Herbert Silberer: Sketches to his life and work. *The Importance of Sexuality in the Work of Sigmund Freud*. Retrieved July 13, 2015 from www.werkblatt.at/nitzschke/text/silberer.htm.

Nunberg, H. & Federn, E. (eds.) (1962) *Minutes of the Vienna Psychoanalytic Society* (Vols 1–4). Translator M. Nunberg, New York: International Universities Press.

Rapaport, D. (1951) *Organization and Pathology of Thought*, New York: Columbia University Press.

Roazen, P. (1984) *Freud and His Followers*, Washington Square, New York: New York University Press.

Silberer, H. (1903) *Viertausend Kilometer im Ballon*. Translator Z. Galsi (2017). Berlin: Heidelberg GmbH: Springer-Verlag, pp. i–ii.

Silberer, H. (1914) Der Homunculus. Translator Z. Galsi. *Imago* 3, pp. 37–79. (Translated version, 2017, pp. 1–48).

Silberer, H. (1919) *Der Traum: Einfuhrung in die Traumpsychologie*. Translator Z. Galsi (2017). Stuttgart: Verlag von Ferdinand Enke.

Silberer, H. (1920) The Origin and the Meaning of the Symbols of Freemasonry. *Psyche and Eros*. Vol. I, No. 1, July 1920, pp. 17–24.

Silberer, H. (1920) Dr. Ernest Jones (London): The Theory of Symbolism. *Psyche and Eros*. Vol I, No, 1, July 1920, pp. 53–57.

Silberer, H. (1920) II. The Symbolism of Building. *Psyche and Eros*. Vol. I, No. 2, September–October 1920, pp. 84–97.

Silberer, H. (1920) The Steinach in Mythology. *Psyche and Eros*. Vol. I, No. 3, November–December 1920, pp. 137–139.

Silberer, H. (1921) III. Sacred Numbers. *Psyche and Eros*. Vol. II., No. 2., March–April 1921, pp. 81–89.

Silberer, H. (1921) Beyond Psychoanalysis. *Psyche and Eros*. Vol. II, No. 3, May–June 1921, pp. 142–151.

Silberer, H. (1921) Jones, Dr. E. (London): The Theory of Symbolism. *Psyche and Eros*. Vol. II, No. 4, July–August 1921, p. 249.

Silberer, H. (1921) The Symbols of Freemasonry. *Psyche and Eros*. Vol. II, No. 5, September–October 1921, pp. 299–309.

Silberer, H. (1922) Sociology, Politics, and Psycho-Analysis. *Psyche and Eros*. Vol. III, No. 1, January–February 1922, pp. 55–61.

Silberer, H. (1922) Freud, Prof. Sigm. Crowd Psychology and Ego-analysis. *Psyche and Eros*. Vol. III, No. 2, March–April 1922, pp. 112–116.

Silberer, H. (1951) Report on a method of eliciting and observing certain symbolic hallucination-phenomena. In *Organization and Pathology of Thought* (pp. 195–207). Editor and translator D. Rapaport. New York: Columbia University Press.

Silberer, H. (1951) On symbol formation. In *Organization and Pathology of Thought* (pp. 208–233). Editor and translator D. Rapaport. New York: Columbia University Press.

Silberer, H. (1955) The dream: Introduction to the psychology of dreams. *The Psychoanalytic Review*. Translator J. Blauner. January 1, 1955; 42, ProQuest, pp. 361–387.

Silberer, H. (2015) *Problems of Mysticism and Its Symbolism* (reprint of 1917). Translator E. Jelliffe. New York: Moffat, Yard and Company.

Weiss, J. & Sampson, H. (1986) *The Psychoanalytic Process: Theory, Clinical Observations, and Empirical Research*, New York: The Guilford Press.

Whitmont, E. C. & Perera, S. B. (1989) *Dreams, A Portal to the Source*, New York: Routledge.

Index

psychoanalytic perspective 26, 27, 30, 31; putrefaction (blackening) and procreation theories 26–27, 30; regeneration theme 24, 27; *The Sphinx* story 29–31; 'spirit in a bottle' notion 28; Viennese alchemical society's fraudulent activities 28

Human Potential Movement 67

Humanistic ('Third Force') Psychology 67

hypnagogic phenomena: autosymbolic phenomena 10–12, 16, 45, 46, 48–49; and dreams 44–46, 48–49; vs Freudian dream theory 12–13; functional (effort) phenomena 6, 11, 12, 44, 48–49, 57; material (content) phenomena 6, 10, 11, 44, 48–49, 57; Rosicrucian parable analysis 57; somatic phenomena 11, 12, 44, 49; work published in *Jahrbuch* journal 8, 10; work translated and footnoted by Rappaport (1951) 10, 13; work well received by Freud 8, 13, 66

idealism 19, 38, 51–52, 65

improvement theme, and the homunculus 26, 31

incest 31, 54; *see also* Oedipal Complex

Integrative Psychology 67

introversion, and rebirth/spirituality/mysticism 40–41

Jahrbuch (journal) 8, 10

Jewish 'Cabala' 33, 37

John's Gospel: death and new life (24:12) 40; story of Nicodemus 40

Jones, Ernest: on Silberer's 'philosophical virus' 9, 65; Silberer's review of *The Theory of Symbolism* 7, 60

Jung, Carl G.: archetypes 42; association experiments 16–17; complexes 17; complexity of his writings 2; dream theory 53, 56, 67; introversion 40; *Jahrbuch* journal editor 8; Oedipal Complex 41, 42;

procreation themes and alchemy 27; on Silberer's discovery of link between alchemy and unconscious 23, 66; symbols 14; symbols and unconscious 58; and Vienna Psychoanalytic Society 1

Kant, Immanuel 10, 33, 58

Keller, Ludwig 35

Kohut, H. 53, 67

Kolnai, A., "Psycho-analysis and Sociology" 61, 62

Krauss, F. S. 7

Ladd, Trumbull 45

Le Bon, Gustave, *The Psychology of Crowds* 62

Leade, Jane 58

'leading edge' concept 67

lecanomancy experiments 41

libido 38, 39, 40

Lorenz, Emil, "The Political Myth, Problem, and Preliminary Communications" 61

Maab, I. G. E. 46

mandrake root 28–29, 31

Masonic symbolism: appraisal of Silberer's work 67; building symbolism (lecture II) 35–37; 'capacity' concept and symbols 34; death and light symbols 38–40; defining symbols (lecture I) 33–35; 'elementary types' theory 41; Freemason symbolism four lectures 7, 32–33, 41–42; Freemasonry, symbols of (lecture IV) 38–41; Freemasonry and alchemy 22, 25, 38, 39; Freemasonry and Rosicrucianism 32; Freud's 'libido' concept revised 38, 39; Kant's categories and historical examples 33; lecanomancy experiments 41; numbers and symbolism (lecture III) 37–38; Oedipus Complex and Jung vs Freud 41, 42; rebirth, introversion and mysticism 40–41; The Royal Art 25, 36, 38, 39, 56, 58–59; Scripture and symbolism 36; superstition 33; threshold symbolism 41

Printed in the United States
by Baker & Taylor Publisher Services